THE
CITIZEN OF INDIA

THE CITIZEN OF INDIA

BY

W. LEE-WARNER , C.S.I., M.A.

GYAN

Published by

GYAN

Gyan Publishing House
5, Ansari Road
Daryaganj, New Delhi-110002
Phone: 011-47034999, 9811692060
E-mail: books@gyanbooks.com

Distribution Network
gyanbooks.com
India, USA, Canada, UK, Australia

ISBN: 978-93-6208-469-9 (HB)
First Published, 1897

2nd Impression 2024

Printed at: Gyan Press, Delhi.

THE CITIZEN OF INDIA
Author: W. LEE-WARNER

THE CITIZEN OF INDIA

H.M. KING EDWARD VII., EMPEROR OF INDIA.

THE
CITIZEN OF INDIA

BY

SIR WILLIAM LEE-WARNER, K.C.S.I.

FELLOW OF THE UNIVERSITY OF BOMBAY, AND FORMERLY ACTING DIRECTOR OF PUBLIC INSTRUCTION IN BERAR AND BOMBAY, AND MEMBER OF THE EDUCATION COMMISSION, 1882-83

REVISED EDITION

MACMILLAN AND CO., LIMITED
ST. MARTIN'S STREET, LONDON
1907

CONTENTS.

CHAPTER I.

CITIZENS AND THEIR RIGHTS.

Rights and duties—Citizens—India—A land of peace—A land of freedom—Queen Victoria's proclamation, - - pp. 1-9

CHAPTER II.

THE VILLAGE.

Common interests—Elements of union in India—The village community—The past and the present—Faults and benefits of the old system—The modern village—Villages share in the benefits of the empire—Personal duty, - - - pp. 9-24

CHAPTER III.

TOWNS AND CITIES.

Urban population—Modern towns—Advantages of towns—Municipal towns—Local boards—The cities—Calcutta—Bombay—Madras—Rangoon—Other capital cities, - - pp. 24-43

CHAPTER IV.

PROVINCES.

Provinces—British provinces—Government of the provinces—Madras—Bombay—Bengal—The United Provinces of Agra and

Oudh—The Punjab—Burma—The Central Provinces and Berar—Eastern Bengal and Assam—The North-West Frontier Province—Ajmer-Merwara—Coorg—British Baluchistan—The Andamans, - - - - - - - - - pp. 44-59

CHAPTER V.

THE NATIVE STATES.

Foreign territory—A difficult task—Policy of non-interference—Subsidiary alliances—A return to the "Let alone" policy—A general protectorate—Misrule and annexation—Adoptions allowed—Classes of states—Rajputana—Central India Agency—Baluchistan—Kathiawar—Hyderabad—Kashmir—Mysore—Baroda—Other states—Advantages of native rule, - pp. 59-76

CHAPTER VI.

THE DISTRICT.

Districts—Districts parts of the province—Area of the district—The district officers—The executive—The collector—Majesty of the law—Duties and powers of the collector—The collector's assistants—Other district officers—Divisions and commissioners—Taluks or parts of the district, - - - - pp. 77-91

CHAPTER VII.

THE SUPREME GOVERNMENT.

Government: central and local—Why there should be supreme control—Supreme rule difficult in former times—The Viceroy—The Executive Council of the Viceroy—The Viceroy's Legislative Council—The Secretariat—Headquarters of the Viceroy—Government in public—Imperial duties—Foreign Affairs—Military and marine forces—Other work of the supreme government—Provincial governments—The Secretary of State for India in Council, - - - - - - pp. 91-113

CHAPTER VIII.

LEGISLATION.

The making of laws—The Council's Acts—Right of interpellation—Special ordinances, - - - - - - pp. 113-119

CHAPTER IX.

RACES AND POPULATION OF INDIA.

What makes a country strong and prosperous?—Famine less to be feared now than formerly—Position of India—Diversities of race—The population—Dangers which beset India, pp. 120-134

CHAPTER X.

TRADES AND OCCUPATIONS OF INDIA.

Division of Labour—Capital—Occupations—Mines—Tea and coffee—Cotton—Other industries—Government service—Emigration and factory laws—The value of freedom, - pp. 135-152

CHAPTER XI.

THE PUBLIC PEACE.

How the peace is kept at home and abroad—Past and present—Naval power—Naval defence of India—The army—Armies of Native states—Civil police—The policeman's finger—Additional police—The people, - - - - - - pp. 153-166

CHAPTER XII

THE PUBLIC HEALTH.

Science—Ignorance—Hospitals—Lady Dufferin—Prevention of disease—Vaccination—Water supply—Conservancy and drainage—Sanitary boards—How government fights famine—Weather forecasts—Irrigation canals—Wells—Railways—Forests—Freedom of trade—Work and charity—Plague—Public markets. - - - - - - - - - pp. 166-186

CHAPTER XIII.

PUBLIC INCOME AND EXPENDITURE.

Taxes, and why we pay them--Public Income—Budget Estimates and Accounts—Taxes and rates—Rules by which taxes are fixed—Total public income—Public expenditure—Gross expenditure—Net expenditure—Credit of India—Exchange, pp. 186-212

CHAPTER XIV.

EDUCATION, JUSTICE AND PUBLIC WORKS.

A choice of benefits—Educational agencies—Public justice—Public works—Railways—Irrigation works—Post office and telegraph—The Press and literature—Education—Government colleges and schools—Private enterprise—Primary education—Numbers being educated, - - - - - - pp. 213-232

CHAPTER XV.

THE TRADE OF INDIA.

Trade a proof of prosperity—Total Trade of India—Bills of Exchange—Imports—Exports—Manufactures make a country rich, - - - - - - - - - - pp. 232-241

CHAPTER XVI.

THE QUEEN'S PROCLAMATION, - - - - - pp. 242-246

LIST OF ILLUSTRATIONS.

	PAGE
H.M. King Edward VII., Emperor of India,	*Frontispiece*
Native Indian Village, - - - - - - -	10
Ruined Temples, Vijayanagar, - - - - -	26
Calcutta, - - - - - - - - - -	35
Bombay from the top of the Clock Tower, - -	39
Madras, - - - - - - - - - - -	41
Lord Clive, - - - - - - - - -	49
Sir Thomas Roe, - - - - - - - -	50
Lord Dufferin, - - - - - - - -	55
Lord Wellesley, - - - - - - - -	62
A Raja of Rajputana, - - - - - - -	69
Nizam-ul-Mulk, - - - - - - - -	71
Charles I. of England, - - - - - -	85
Walter Hospital, - - - - - - - -	89
Types of the British Army, - - - - - -	94
Types of Indian Cavalry, - - - - - -	95
Lord Minto, - - - - - - - - -	99
One of the Viceroy's Bodyguard, - - - -	107
Houses of Parliament, London, - - - - -	111

PAGE

A Naga Chief, - - - - - - - - - 126

A Rajput Warrior, - - - - - - - 129

Gurkha Soldiers, - - - - - - - - 133

Banjaras, - - - - - - - - - 137

Indian Ploughman (Madras), - - - - - 141

Cotton going to the Mill, - - - - - - 146

Nelson, - - - - - - - - - - 155

Officers and Men of the British Navy, - - - 157

A Calcutta Policeman, - - - - - - - - 164

Lord Lister, - - - - - - - - - - 169

Lady Dufferin, - - - - - - - - - 172

The Three Canals, Bezwada, - - - - - 178

Taj Mahal, - - - - - - - - - - 189

Railway Bridge across the Jumna, - - - - 208

Madras Law Courts, - - - - - - - - 220

Aqueduct, Ganges Canal, - - - - - - 223

Postman, Bombay, - - - - - - - - 225

Senate House, Madras, - - - - - - - - 229

CITIZEN OF INDIA

CHAPTER I.

CITIZENS AND THEIR RIGHTS.

1. **Rights and duties.** When we begin to talk of citizens or to read about them, we shall often hear of 'rights' and 'duties.' Let us try to understand the meaning of these words. If I *owe* anybody money or anything else it is my *duty* to pay it to him, and he has a *right* to demand payment from me. As we grow up from childhood to manhood, at each stage of our lives we keep on finding out how much we owe to others, and fresh duties are constantly being added to our list of debts. We learn at home our first lesson on duty—to honour and obey our parents—and we have a right to expect that they will support, educate, and love us, because we are their own children. At school we are taught not merely to obey our masters, but also to be kind and polite to the pupils who attend it. From the school or college we pass into the outside world, where we meet with persons who do not belong to our family and never attended our school. They are strangers to us, and yet we owe them duties. Some men may earn a

livelihood by tilling the soil, others by keeping shops, and others again by various industries and occupations. He who tills the soil, the cultivator, has the right to expect that his crops will not be injured by travellers or stolen by thieves, and that the supply of water which belongs to him will not be turned aside or wasted by others. But he ought to treat others as he expects them to treat him. It is his duty, therefore, to respect the rights of his neighbours in these matters. The shopkeeper buys and sells goods. When he buys, he looks for honest dealing and proper weights, and it is his duty when he sells to deal fairly with others. And in whatever way we may earn a living, all of us find that peace and freedom are necessary for our happiness and prosperity.

It is the duty of our government to secure these blessings for us. The roads which we use ought to be kept in order and free from robbers; dispensaries and hospitals are needed for the sick; Courts of Justice should be provided to punish wrong-doers and settle disputes; and armed forces are required to keep off our enemies. Those whose business it is to spend time and money in these matters have the right to collect from the people the taxes and rates which are spent upon the public objects. At times also it may be necessary that we ourselves should help in suppressing disorders. Thus we see how our rights and duties extend beyond our homes and villages. But besides duties to our fellow-countrymen, we have duties to our neighbours in foreign countries.

There was a time when the tribesmen on the north western frontier of India often used to attack Indian villages and carry off not only the property of the people but also their women and children. In revenge, the Indian villagers attacked the tribesmen, and the border-land became so disturbed that large tracts of good land were left waste. To prevent disorders of this kind, the Government placed agents in foreign territory, and entered into treaties and engagements with its rulers. It is the duty of every one who lives in India to carry out the agreements thus made, and it is his right to expect that foreign rulers will perform their promises. Thus it appears that our rights and duties are not confined even to India itself. We owe something not only to our families, our fellow-countrymen, and our government, but also to neighbouring nations, because we live in India.

2. **Citizens.** The first meaning of the word *citizen* is 'one who lives in a city.' When men began to live together in cities they soon understood the meaning of rights and duties and the need for keeping on good terms with their neighbours. So long as families or tribes of men lived apart from other tribes, hiding in the dense forests, or wandering over the plains where they pleased, and moving from one place to another in search of fresh pasture for their flocks, or new fields to cultivate, they thought of no duties outside themselves or their tribes. In course of time some of them gave up their wandering life and settled down at one spot. They built themselves houses and formed villages, cultivating the lands near them. But when they had stored up their crops and increased their cattle, often other tribes attacked them and robbed

them of their goods. The villagers were at first too few to protect themselves, and they therefore sought shelter in larger villages or towns. The towns became the residences of nobles or chiefs, who adorned them with fine buildings and fortified them with walls and ditches; they protected the inhabitants of the cities, and, in turn, the citizens were required to perform various duties and pay taxes. As cities grew in population they depended more and more upon the surrounding country to supply them with food, wood, clothing, and various other things. Villages and cities therefore united with the inhabitants of the country outside their walls, and thus formed districts, sharing their rights and duties with others. In this way the inhabitants of one country, under one government, became citizens of a state.

So long as the government was able to protect them and treated the people fairly the country remained united, but in former times the different countries of India were under many rulers, and the chiefs and ruling families were constantly at war with one another. Districts and whole provinces often changed masters, so that the subjects of many states could not get attached to their rulers or become as fond of their country as the dwellers in cities are of their own city. But now, for more than a century, the greater part of India, although its districts may have been attached to this or that province according to convenience, has enjoyed one and the same British Government. The people have been blessed with peace, and have learnt to think of justice and liberty as their rights. As men formerly spoke of a citizen of Delhi or Lucknow, so now they speak of "citizens of India," meaning the residents of this vast country united by one government, enjoying the same rights, and owing the same duties to their fellow-subjects and to the King Emperor who protects them all in their liberties.

3. **India.** The country of which we are citizens to-day is one of which we have good reason to be proud. Its snow-clad mountains in the north are the most lofty in the world; its rivers are famous for their length and size; its fertile plains are covered with rich crops; and its forests contain valuable timber, which supplies the markets of the world. Travellers by railway can see that the country owes very much of its fertility to its great rivers. There are in India forty-five railway bridges more than a quarter of a mile long, twenty-five more than half a mile, ten more than three-quarters of a mile, one more than a mile and a quarter, two more than a mile and a half each, and one more than one and three quarters of a mile in length. There are forty-four millions of acres watered by canals, tanks, and wells. There are splendid harbours on the coast, and metalled roads over all parts of the country. The area of India exceeds 1,766,000 square miles, and the people number 294 millions. Beneath the soil are hidden stores of gold, precious stones, iron, coal and other minerals, all ready to be used in the service of its citizens.

Many races of men possessing different qualities and of different religions inhabit it. In past ages, there have lived here great poets, law-givers, warriors and heroes of mighty fame, and kings whose palaces, tombs, and public buildings still adorn the cities in which their builders lived. It is a free country, in which the people are allowed to write or say what they like, to meet together, and to live where they please, so long as they do not break the law. Trade and commerce flourish, and although famine and plague at times visit the land, its population and wealth are continually growing.

4. **A land of peace.** India has passed through many trials and changes of government in the past. If you take any district that you please, you will see at once that without peace the citizens cannot increase in numbers, nor can they make full use of the advantages which they possess in their noble country. In the united provinces of Agra and Oudh there is a district named Bulandshahr which enjoyed much prosperity under the rule of Akbar and his successors. When the Moghal empire was broken up the peace of the district was destroyed; the fields ceased to be tilled because no man could be sure that he would reap what he had sown; and the villages were deserted because the lives and property of the people were not safe. The famine of 1783 reduced even the people of the towns to starvation, and many poor citizens sold themselves or their families into slavery for the sake of a few meals.

At the beginning of last century the district came under the rule of the East India Company, and order was restored. In 1848 a little more than a half of the whole area of Bulandshahr was being cultivated, and the inhabitants numbered 700,000. In 1871, the cultivated area had risen to 64 per cent. of the area fit for tillage, and the population to 936,000. In 1890, another addition of five per cent. was made to the land under culture, and the citizens numbered 950,000. At the beginning of this century 73 per cent. of the whole area was giving crops, and the people had increased to 1,138,100 souls. Their houses are built of better material, their cattle have increased, and the quality of their food has improved. The wages of artizans have risen, and mills for pressing and cleaning cotton have been introduced. The history of this district is that of many others in all parts of the country. Where peace and liberty are enjoyed, the citizens increase, fresh industries are started, and, as a consequence, the people enjoy more rights, and their duties grow with their rights.

5. **A land of freedom**. Something else besides peace is needed so that the citizens of a great country may make the best use of the resources which they enjoy. There are many countries in which the citizens are not allowed to leave the villages in which they were born, nor to seek elsewhere such employment as they please. It was so once in India, and for ages Indian labourers, artizans, and tradesmen used to follow the trades of their fathers whether they liked to do so or not. In many countries of Europe men are to-day compelled to serve in the army for a short time in order that they may be able to fight for their country when their services are required.

In India there used to be forced labour, and the roads or canals were repaired by compelling men in many cases to work upon them without wages. In the matter of trade heavy taxes were put upon certain articles, so that people could not afford to buy what they wanted. Tolls were taken from those who used the roads and bridges, and transit duties were charged upon goods which passed between the interior and the seaports. As people could not move about as they pleased or convey goods from one place to another, the cost of living was much higher than it need have been, and the people were prevented from using their labour in such employments as they chose. In some places, and at some times, a special tax was put upon those who professed certain religions, as in the case of the *jizia* imposed upon the Hindus, which the Emperor Akbar removed and Aurangzib reimposed. Even now the rulers of many countries in the East try to prevent their citizens making use of the wonderful machines and discoveries which have been introduced into the western world, such as railways, the telegraph, the steam engine, and electricity. In all these matters India enjoys not only peace, but also liberty, freedom of person, freedom of action and speech, and freedom of movement and trade.

6. **Queen Victoria's proclamation.** In the year 1857 the government of our country passed from the hands of a number of British merchants, known as the United East India Company, into those of the ruler of the United Kingdom. The Queen of Great Britain and Ireland became the Queen of British India, and in the year 1876 she assumed the title of Queen-Empress of India. One of the first acts of the Queen of India was to send a royal message to her subjects in this country, which is printed in full at the end of

this book. She assured them that her strength would be in the prosperity of her Indian subjects, her security in their contentment, and that their gratitude would be regarded by Her Majesty as her best reward. She gave them liberties such as few other nations in the world enjoy, and when in 1901 our King-Emperor Edward VII. ascended the throne, he repeated the promises so graciously given by his sovereign mother.

The citizens of India are citizens of the British Empire, which extends to all parts of the earth, so that the sun never sets upon the whole of it. Whatever fame and honour belong to this Empire now belong to us as its citizens. We all share in the peace and freedom which God has granted to its subjects. East and west, India and England, are joined together, and while it is the right of every citizen of India to enjoy the liberties of the British subject, it is also his duty to take his part in preserving those liberties and handing them on to his children.

CHAPTER II.

THE VILLAGE.

7. **Common interests.** The house is the home of the family, and in it the various members, each and all, learn and practise their duties towards one another. In the same way the village is the home of the

citizen. It is in the village that the greatest numbers of the people of India live. In it men of various families, races, and religions, engaged in different trades and occupations, feel that they must work for and with one another because they live together in the same village. In other words, they find that they are united by *a common interest.* A similar lesson is taught in the town or city where the popula-

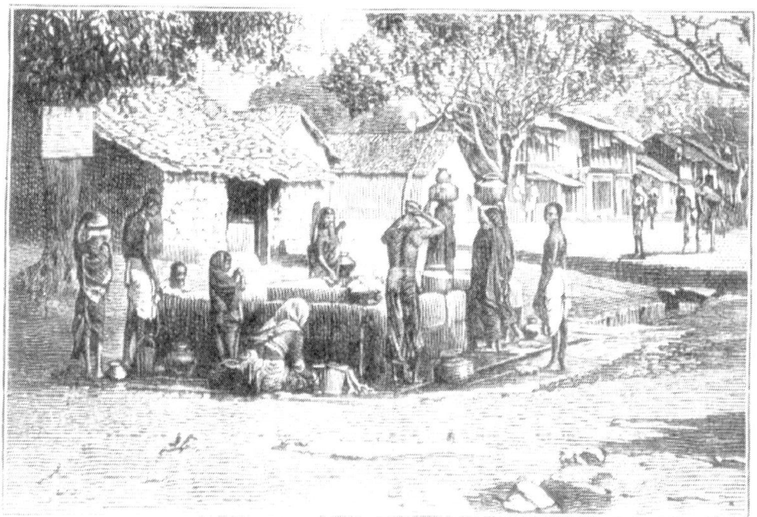

NATIVE INDIAN VILLAGE.

tion is larger and the duties of the citizens more numerous. There are in the whole of India only 2,150 towns, but there are more than 728,600 villages, and in the latter 265 millions of persons live. It is in villages that most of the citizens of India enjoy their rights and perform their duties to one another.

The first lesson learned in these villages is that a man may belong to another caste or religion, and may be engaged in a different trade from that followed by his neighbour, and yet be to him a good fellow-citizen. He may leave his fellows to obey their rules of caste or the teachings of their own religions, and yet take his share of the work of the village by their sides, and help them to preserve their liberties and rights.

The second lesson learned there is that the more we know about our neighbours and the laws and rules of our Government, the more ready shall we be to keep on friendly terms, and to join together in working for the common good. We ourselves must suffer if others should be afflicted with the plague, or if they should break the laws, or destroy the public property. We are all interested in the health, peace, and prosperity of our own village.

We have, in fact, common interests; and if any one should ask what is meant by common interests, he cannot do better than think of his own body. The body consists of different parts, and if one part suffers pain all the members suffer with it. If, for instance, the finger of a man is hurt, we say that he has a pain in his finger. So too in the case of a larger community of towns and villages, if one village, or town, suffers from plague, famine, or other disaster, the whole province feels the pain in all its villages and towns; and if the province suffers, the whole nation suffers with it. The interests of one part are the interests of all, and we shall presently see that there are many things which each of us desires to see done, and which we can only get done by the action of several men working together. Thus, the canal which brings water to one or more villages can only be made at a heavy cost which all other villages must help to bear; and the roads and railways which many of us use are constructed by the united effort of the whole population.

8. **Elements of union in India.** It is a common saying that 'unity is strength,' and the division of India into so large a number of small villages sometimes makes it difficult to unite its scattered citizens. In Europe the feeling of patriotism is promoted by wars carried on against a national enemy, by the combination of many citizens for social or political purposes, by the large number and size of the towns and cities, by trade or commerce, and by travel and intercourse. Although there are some differences of religion and race amongst the inhabitants of European countries, yet the great majority of them are Christians, and the customs and habits of the various classes of society are very similar. In India these influences tending towards union are often wanting. But, on the other hand, the inhabitants have from the earliest times possessed certain traits of character and customs likely to draw them together, which western countries have lacked. Personal devotion to a chief, obedience to the father of a family, a strong sense of religion, and village communities have, in the past, laid in India a foundation for useful citizenship. The people have long since felt in the family circle, in the religious sect, or in village life, the practical advantages of common action. To a large extent men have been accustomed to look beyond themselves, and to feel that they are members of a wider circle than that of their own separate families.

The village and the caste system have thus introduced into the daily life of the country an idea of co-operation, and a feeling that, if one caste of labourers supplies one want of the village or the nation, its wants should be supplied in turn by other castes. The spirit of mutual helpfulness, and the sense, shared by all classes, of dependence upon government and a higher providence, are influences which even to-day tend to unite the people of India. On the other hand, the very system of family, caste, and creed which has fostered them, is sometimes apt to keep these influences to a narrow circle. The natives of India are famed for their charity, but their charity is more confined within the caste or the sect than is the case in Europe. The citizen ought to have a wider range of duties and privileges than any class or sect of the community can have. As the family is merged in the village, so the village is merged in the province, and the province in the empire, and by the term 'citizens' we mean the people of a whole empire united under one government, sharing liberties and rights in common, and owing duties not only to their own castemen or fellow-villagers, but to the whole body of their fellow-countrymen.

9. **The village community**. There are nearly 56 million houses in Indian villages and towns. The number of villages in the whole of India, including the native states, is 728,600, and they may be divided into three different classes. In the first place, new villages spring up every year as the population of the country increases, or as water is carried by canals into parts of the country which used to be desert. The

process of making new villages has been going on continually for the last hundred years in many parts of the country, and for only a few years in other parts more recently annexed to British India. But there is one feature common to all these modern villages. Growing up in safety and under the protection of British laws, they have not required either the outward defences or the local administration which villagers needed in the days of disturbance before the establishment of order and peace.

The older villages of the country may be divided into two classes according to the systems which have prevailed in them from former days, namely, the raiyatwari and the joint-village system. It is easy to understand how the raiyatwari village came into existence. In the earliest times a family settled down in a particular spot and tilled the soil. The head of the family was the ruler of the house, and, when his children married and built themselves houses, his authority extended over all. Gradually other families came to reside in the neighbourhood, and they built their houses near to the first comers as a matter of safety and convenience. They soon found it necessary to employ servants for the benefit of the whole village, such as the barber, the carpenter, the blacksmith, the washerman, the potter, and in course of time the silver-smith and the copper-smith. The cultivators ploughed the land, gathered the crops, and, after paying the rent due to the ruler of the country, they supported the village priests and the temple servants, rewarding the village artizans for their services by giving them a share of the produce according to custom.

Between the raiyats and the officers of Government there stood generally a descendant of the family which had first settled there, the village 'headman,' who collected the rents due to the Government, and an accountant who recorded the amounts; they being granted lands rent free, with contributions from the raiyats. The first thing which had to be thought about was the protection of the village against robbers. For this reason a wall, a stockade, or a fence of prickly pear was constructed round the village, and the gates were guarded at night by the village watchman. When disputes between the villagers had to be settled, the matter was referred to a *panchayat* or local council. The officers of the Government took care that their share of the produce was paid, but for the rest they spent nothing upon the villagers, leaving even the roads and tanks to be provided for by the people themselves. Villages on the raiyatwari system are found in most parts of the Dekhan and Southern India.

In the Punjab and Northern India the joint-village system prevails. There, as the raiyats who actually cultivate the soil do not separately pay their rents to Government, a single village headman is not required. The lands belong to heads of families who have shares in the village and manage its affairs by a council. It is supposed that, in times past, the ancestors of these shareholders either drove the original settlers out of the village, or else took from them their lands and compelled them to labour for their new masters. In any case the new comers required help to carry on the business of the village, and were obliged to employ artizans, village watchmen, and other servants.

Thus in the old days of disorder the inhabitants alike of raiyatwari, and of other villages on the joint-village system, arranged amongst themselves for the conduct of their local affairs. Some tilled the soil, while others undertook the protection of the village, or the manufacture of simple articles needed by the cultivators and their families, for which they were paid by a share of the produce.

10. **The past and the present.** Just as the villages which have been founded in the last century differ from the older village communities, so also have changes taken place in those ancient communities themselves. The inhabitants of raiyatwari and other ancient villages have no need to-day for walls, stockades, or fences to protect them from attack at night. Even the great cities which had fortifications and splendid gates, such as those of Delhi and Ahmedabad, have now thrown down their walls and ramparts, and spread out into the open country. The seat of government in Calcutta used to be known as Fort William, that in Madras as Fort St. George, and that in Bombay as the Castle. It is difficult now even to trace the ruins of the walls which once surrounded them. The villages, as well as the towns and cities of India, are protected from attack by other means, and the walls which hindered the free movements of the people are not needed in a time of peace and order.

It is, moreover, good for the health of the inhabitants that the fresh air should have free entrance into their dwellings. An eminent doctor has lately expressed the opinion that the plague has been more severe and its ravages more prolonged in those parts of the country where the villages are still to some extent confined by fences and walls. This was also the experience of England when in 1665 the great plague, or the black death, devastated London and other parts of England. The narrow ill-ventilated streets, the want of drainage, and absence of pure air from the houses of the inhabitants, encouraged the spread of the disease, and the great Fire of London was not without its advantages in removing ill-built streets into which fresh air and light could not find their way.

The spirit which distinguishes the present from the past in India is that of freedom. The old walls of the villages have been broken down in more senses than one. The raiyats and the artizans may go where they like and when they please. The roads are kept in order without forced labour, the prices at which food-stuff and other articles may be sold are free from all law or regulation, and all classes and persons may bring their complaints before the courts of justice. The villager is not confined to his village; his interests extending to the district or province to which he belongs. He is in reality a citizen of a great country with rights and duties that extend far beyond the circle of the small community in which he was born. It is well to understand how this great change has come about in the lives of the people and what it means. Without a strong and just government at the head of affairs it would be impossible for the residents of nearly three quarters of a million of villages to arrange matters so that all might be able to work together for the defence of their country and enjoy the fruits of peace and order.

11. **Faults and benefits of the old system** We need not find fault with the villagers of old days because they shut themselves up behind walls and thought only of their own local interests. Mountstuart Elphinstone, who was governor of Bombay in 1820, remarked that the village communities were "an excellent remedy for the imperfections of a bad form of government," and that they "prevented the bad effects of its negligences and weakness." When the rulers of a province spent nothing upon its defences and its roads, it was wise on the part of the villages to protect themselves, and to gather within their walls the labourers and artizans required for their daily wants. Since no courts of law were provided, it was well that disputes should be settled by a *panchayat*. But when a foreign invader, such as Nadir Shah, came down to rob the inhabitants of the plains and cities of India it was soon found that villages, however well protected by their inhabitants, were quite unable to drive back his powerful armies.

So too when the Pindaris and other gangs of robbers within India itself went forth to pillage and destroy their own country, each village perished as the hosts of thieves advanced. At times the residents of a large town, like Guntur, preferred to set fire to their houses and perish with their families in the flames rather than submit to the cruelties of such cut-throats. The villages endured these sufferings in times of war or disturbance, because they had not arranged with other villages for their common defence.

Instead of combining to send forth an army to defeat the foe at a distance from their houses they waited at home until they were attacked and plundered, one after another.

Such was the result of want of union in time of war; but even in times of peace the whole country suffered other miseries, because each village lived for itself. When famine or pestilence visited the land, the Government seldom did anything to save the lives and properties of the afflicted masses. It sometimes carried away what it could of the scanty crops, and left the villagers to starve. The cultivators were no longer able to pay the usual dues to the village servants, and many of these helpless people died of starvation, while others sold themselves or their children as slaves to any one who would feed them. If only the villagers in all parts of India had combined with one another, they might have arranged for those villages in which famine prevailed to draw their supplies of food from distant provinces, and paid for them in times of plenty and good crops. But so long as each village stood alone, it was as weak in times of distress as a single stick taken from a bundle, or a single strand torn from a strong rope.

12. **The modern village.** The villages have lost nothing by the changes which have taken place in the government of India. Many of them still keep the names which they had in the distant past, and occupy the same sites. Traces still exist of their ancient constitution. In raiyatwari villages the headman, or patel, performs his public duties and exercises an authority in revenue and in police

matters over the other residents. He has his colleague, the village accountant, known as the kulkarni, the patwari, or the karnam, who keeps the accounts and writes the returns required by government. Although the village-servants may go where they please, they frequently continue to perform their usual duties, and prefer to remain where their fathers lived.

But the events of their daily lives ought to remind the villagers that they are citizens of an empire whose rulers provide for their wants and safety, and expect them in turn to assist in making their country strong and prosperous. The postman brings to their doors letters from all parts of the country; the officers of the district and provincial courts of justice are to be seen in their midst; the district engineer inspects their roads; the educational inspectors examine their schools; and the collector of the district with his assistants visits their fields. A district police force arrests robbers and thieves and removes criminals from their midst. At times a military force passes through the country, and every one hears of expeditions undertaken against the wild tribes on the Indian frontier to punish them for raids upon Indian villages. Thus with the roads safe there is much coming and going, and freed from the necessity of defending their own villages the people live securely and reap the crops which they have grown.

It is not necessary for the people to provide for their safety by leaving the country and dwelling in the large cities. In fact, the village population still vastly exceeds in numbers the town population, for in calculating the latter it is usual to take a collection of houses in which 5000 or more people live as constituting a town and not a village. Reckoning in this way, nine persons out of ten in the whole of India dwell in villages, and only one in ten lives in towns or cities. But the village population varies in different provinces. In Bengal it is as high as 95 per cent. and in Bombay as low as 81 per cent. The average number of souls in an Indian village also varies considerably. In Burma the population of the villages averages 157, in Bengal 335, in Bombay 508, and in Madras 623 souls. One half of all the villages in the empire contain less than 200 residents. Taking the whole country we find on an average a village in every two-and-a-half square miles, but in Bengal there is one to be found in every square mile, while in Sindh the average is one village in every twelve square miles.

Thus it will be seen that India is still a land of villages and its population rural. Although these inhabitants are scattered over the whole face of the empire in small communities, without the protection of walls or fences, they are perfectly safe, and dwell in peace. They are scattered, but a strong hand unites them, and as a mighty river is fed by many streams and rivulets, so the villagers contribute to the strength of the whole country and receive in turn their share of the protection and public works which the government extends with equal care to all its subjects. Instead of relying upon themselves alone for their defence and local administration, the inhabitants of each village look to all other villages and towns to provide for the common needs of society, and to government to use the resources of all of them for the common good.

13. Villages share in the benefits of the empire. We often hear the complaint made that Indian villagers have on the one hand lost their old interest in the affairs of their own village, and on the other take no part in the larger concerns of the country of which they are citizens. It is said that they readily felt the need of living for, and, if the necessity arose, of dying for their neighbours in the village, but that they cannot understand how the interests of a village are bound up in those of other villages far from their dwellings, nor what share they have in the misfortunes or the prosperity of the empire. The daily experience of every citizen is enough to supply an answer to these complaints. Although the inhabitants of towns have special rights and privileges which can only be enjoyed in places where the population is large, yet the residents of the smallest villages share equally with the townsmen the rights of protection, freedom, law, and justice.

In old days, as we have seen, the villages were constantly exposed to attack and unable to defend themselves. The raiyat may now dwell secure under his own roof, cultivate his fields, and reap the produce. He may do what he likes so long as he does not break the law, and go where he pleases without asking leave from any one. The courts of law are open to him, and the officers of government dare not treat him unjustly. His produce is carried to market over mighty rivers and through forests along roads which are maintained for his benefit as well as others. Although the rains may fail in an entire province, so that the crops wither and even the grass does not spring up, yet a supply of food will find its way to every village and the people will obtain work or relief from the government while the severe distress lasts. In short, if any villager opens his eyes to what he sees around him, he cannot doubt that the government cares for him and provides for his wants, just as much as it cares for the citizens of the most important towns in the empire.

14. **Personal duty.** Since this is the case, it is the duty of every citizen to think of what is expected from him. The government, while it does not desire that each village should waste its money and labour upon keeping up its own defences, needs the help of all its subjects to provide for the good of all. The character of the public servants depends to a large extent upon the behaviour of each private person. The human body cannot enjoy health if the several members do not work together for it. In the same way the government of a country cannot be carried on if the citizens do not take an active part in assisting it. It is not at all necessary that a man should be in the service of the State in order to fulfil his duty to the State. We hear sometimes complaints of the corruption of the police, of the miscarriage of justice, or of the spread of disease which can be prevented. But bribes would not be taken if they were not offered, injustice would not be done by courts of law if false evidence were not given, and disease would not spread

if it were not first produced and diffused by neglect of proper precautions.

The country has a right to expect that each citizen will use his best endeavours to promote the causes of justice and public health. Within the village community there used to be a spirit of mutual help and service for the common good. Although the circle of our duties is enlarged, there is no reason why the same idea should not animate the residents of a province or a country. In an address delivered in Calcutta in December, 1896, the Honourable Mr. Justice Ranade, C.I.E., made these observations: "The State after all exists only to make individual members composing it nobler, happier, richer, and more perfect in every attribute with which we are endowed: and this perfection of our being can never be insured by any outside arrangement, however excellent, unless the individual member concerned is in himself prepared in his own private social sphere of duties to co-operate in his own well-being."

CHAPTER III.

TOWNS AND CITIES.

15. **Urban population.** The census report gives the number of people in India. It also shows the difference between villages, towns, and cities. A number of people living together in one place make up a *town*, if they amount to 5000 souls or more, and a

village, if their number is less. If the population is 100,000 or more, the town becomes a *city*, and a capital city is the principal town of a province in which the chief offices of Government are placed. The population of both towns and cities is called *urban* from a Latin word *urbs*, which means a town, while that of the villages is called *rural* from the Latin *rus*, which means the country.

The main difference between India and most European countries is that in the former the rural population is very much larger than the urban. In the United Kingdom of Great Britain and Ireland, which is only one-fifteenth of the size of India, a third of the people lives in 39 cities; in Germany a sixth of them lives in 33 cities; and in France a seventh resides in only 15 cities. In England and Wales more than half of the whole nation lives in towns with more than 20,000 inhabitants, while in India not a twentieth part is found in such towns.

In the great Indian empire there are only about 250 towns in which some 15 millions reside, while the number of towns containing 50,000 people is 83, several of them being of modern growth. There are besides 1300 smaller towns, each containing from 5000 to 20,000 inhabitants, and, taking together the residents of all Indian towns, they only amount to 10 per cent. of the whole population. The effect of continued peace is, however, shown in the continuous growth of trade and commerce, which is sure to draw persons from the country to the towns. Owing to this cause the urban population is constantly increasing. Thus in the last ten years the number of cities with

100,000 inhabitants has risen by eight, those with over 50,000 by twelve, and those with over 20,000 by forty-five.

16. **Modern towns.** In the town, as in the village, a change has taken place in the classes of people which live in it and the way in which

RUINED TEMPLES, VIJAYANAGAR.

they live. In the days of old, large cities were either founded by some great chief or king, who lived there with his court and followers, or else they grew up round a famous shrine or temple, which was visited by crowds of pilgrims. The celebrated traveller, Bernier, who visited India in 1659 in the reign of the emperor Aurangzib, thus described what he saw: "A capital city, such as Delhi or Agra, derives its chief support from the presence of the army, and the people have to follow the Moghal whenever he takes a long journey. These cities may be compared to a camp. The king's pay is the only means of support." Whole cities were sometimes ordered to remove themselves to another place at the bidding of the emperor. The most famous and cruel instance of this was the transfer of the capital by Mahomed Tughlak from Delhi to Daulatabad in the fourteenth century, a measure which brought ruin and death to many thousands of the citizens.

Cities were, in fact, nothing more than camps, and the language spoken in and round the capital of the Moghals came to be called *Urdu*, which means a camp. When one king made war upon another the blow fell heavily upon the cities, and thus Delhi was often plundered in former days. On the other hand, the urban population enjoyed the protection of the king's soldiers, and the profits of trade with them. Arms, armour, horses, ornaments, cloth of gold, illuminated manuscripts, jewels, and such articles as the court or the military officers required, were readily sold. A king of fine tastes also encouraged learned men and poets to settle in his capital. Splendid tombs and palaces were built and maintained, giving labour and service to the inhabitants. It is true that much of the labour was got by force, and even skilled workmen were compelled to enter and to remain in the service of the chief and his nobles. Still, work and the means of living were found for many persons, and the taxes paid by the villagers and the cultivators of the soil were often spent for the benefit of the town.

In our day towns are built up in quite a different way. The rural population flocks to the towns to please itself, and to supply the wants not of a few favoured persons, but of the masses of the people. Trade, commerce, and manufactures are the objects which draw together workmen and shopkeepers. Accordingly, some of the old cities which had the advantages of rivers or positions favourable to trade still flourish, such as Delhi and Lucknow. Others—such as Patna, the capital of Chandragupta, more than two thousand years ago; Bijapur, adorned by the Muhammadan kings of the Adil Shahi dynasty in the sixteenth century; Vijayanagar, the splendid capital of the Hindu ruler who restored the kingdom of Carnata in Southern India; and Ajodhya, the capital of Rama in the north—have decayed or are in ruins.

The modern capital cities of India lie upon the coast or on mighty rivers, where the naval power of Great Britain can protect them, and where goods carried by ships along the paths of the sea can reach them. Owing to these advantages Calcutta, Bombay, Rangoon, and Karachi enjoy a prosperity such as Delhi never reached in the day of its grandeur, and yet their names were not even known to the Moghal emperors. The people of the surrounding country flow naturally into them and supply the wants of a vast population, receiving in return wages and the articles of dress and daily use which the villagers require. No large military force, no lavish expenditure of court or nobles create the market. The common people themselves are both purchasers and sellers, exchanging with one another the products of their labour and reaping the profits of it.

17. **Advantages of towns.** The prosperity of the city now depends upon the prosperity of the village, and the citizen of each learns that the interests of the urban and rural population are the same. Stately buildings adorn many cities, and the inhabitants have reason to be proud of the noble tombs, palaces, and public buildings which were raised by former rulers of India. But the country which paid the taxes and bore the cost of these buildings gained little benefit from them. It is otherwise with railways and good roads, which connect the villages with the towns and the towns with the cities of a province. All classes reap the benefit of them. The cultivators can by means of them carry and sell their foodstuffs in the town, and the townspeople pay less for the produce of the villages if the expense of carrying it to town is reduced. In the same way canals are doubly useful, supplying the towns with good drinking water, and the villages with water for their crops.

It has been mentioned in the first chapter that India is a land of peace and freedom, and it has been shown that many things can be done by the united effort of a number of citizens which cannot be undertaken by a few. Towns and cities give to the people an opportunity for gathering together in large groups, and so uniting to carry on large industries. Manufactories for weaving cloth, working iron, and tanning leather are thus established in the larger cities, giving labour to the villagers during those seasons of the year when work cannot be done in the fields.

Fuel, whether wood or coal, is needed in the cities not only for cooking purposes, but also for driving the engines used in factories and lighting the streets at night. These wants in town can only be supplied by working the forests and mines of the country. Thus we see how the good of the village is promoted by the welfare of the town, and the citizens are taught by daily experience that each depends on the other.

18. **Municipal towns.** The assembly of a large number of citizens in a town also enables government to entrust to some of the foremost and best educated of them a share in the public business of the country. Local affairs in which the townsmen are specially interested, such as the care and lighting of their streets, the education of the children, the water-supply, drainage, and conservancy, the maintenance of hospitals or dispensaries, and so forth, are duties which the residents of towns or cities are well able to undertake for themselves. Excluding the four capital cities of Calcutta, Madras, Bombay, and Rangoon, which possess considerable revenues and powers of self-government, there were, in 1903, in British India 756 municipal towns with a total population of about 14 millions; of this number the presidency of Bombay had 166, Bengal 157, the Punjab 137, and the United Provinces 104, while in Madras there were 60 municipalities, the remainder being scattered over the other provinces.

Municipal or local self-government does not mean that those towns which enjoy it cease to be under the general government of the country. They are bound to obey and live by the laws which apply to all citizens of India, and to contribute their share of the taxes, which are paid by all inhabitants of the empire towards the cost of the public safety and the public good. But for a good many other advantages which benefit their own town they are allowed by law to levy rates (or local taxes) upon the population and to spend the proceeds in the town. There is so much work to be done in a large country by the government and its officials that it is wise to secure the assistance of the townspeople in providing for their own wants. In the first place, the local residents are better able to understand what is required in their town than the officers of state who live elsewhere and have to attend to other duties. In the next place, those who exercise a local authority learn for themselves what government means. They see how impossible it is to find money to spend upon all the wants of their fellow citizens. They gain what is called a political education, and are taught by experience some of the difficulties of governing a country.

It is impossible, of course, to give unlimited powers to municipal bodies. Such large concerns as the maintenance of the army or the police forces must be left to the central authorities, who alone can ensure efficiency and economy. Again, even in the matters of local administration, control and supervision are necessary. The levy of new taxes, the raising of loans, and expenditure on very large schemes, require the sanction of government under the Municipal Acts. Nevertheless, municipalities enjoy very real powers and administer considerable revenues through their boards or committees. It is clearly impossible for every townsman to take a personal share in the administration, and accordingly a few of them are formed into boards or committees which undertake the duties for the rest. Nearly 10,200 members of boards, more than half of them being elected by the ratepayers, conducted in 1902-3 the affairs of the four capital cities and the other municipalities in British India; of them 7880 held no public office under government, being called non-official members. While the European members numbered 1340 no less than 8860 Indians held municipal office. It is thus clear that non-officials and natives of India conduct the main part of urban administration, and, ever since 1850, their powers have been growing.

The year 1883 was specially marked in their history as the date from which the election of town councillors took the place of the former system of nomination by government. Some idea may be formed of the importance of urban self-government from the fact that, in the year mentioned above, the expenditure of the 760 boards exceeded 867 lakhs of rupees. This sum, amounting to three rupees for each resident, represented a revenue per head of the municipal population larger even than the average contribution paid to the government by each citizen of India. Thus the townspeople enjoy not only their share of the taxes paid for preserving the peace and improving the public works of India, but also the proceeds of municipal rates and taxes which are spent for their special benefit by their own boards.

19. **Local boards.** We may briefly mention here a further attempt made by the British Government to

give the citizens an interest and a share in their own government. Its success varies much in the different provinces, but nowhere has it been possible to give the rural population the same measure of self-government as that conferred upon municipalities. In the country, as well as in the town, it was thought that committees or boards might be formed to look after primary education, district roads, and dispensaries. Accordingly, more than a thousand local boards have been created with 16,000 members, of whom 5400 are elected. In Madras where the attempt has succeeded better than elsewhere, unions of villages represented by their headmen, with certain other members nominated by government, have been formed and have reached the number of 380 unions. But whereas in a town the municipal members live generally close to each other and are well known to many of their neighbours, the representatives of districts, talukas, or unions are usually strangers to each other, and less inclined to meet and work together. An official chairman is therefore required to direct their proceedings, and rural boards are not likely to prove so successful forms of self-government as municipalities have already become.

For, in the first place, the citizens of a taluka or a district live scattered in many villages apart from each other, and are busily engaged in the cultivation of their fields or the small trades of their village. They have neither the time nor the interest in the affairs of a large tract of country which the dwellers in a town or city have in its affairs. In the second place, the members of the local boards are not only strangers to each other, but they find it difficult to understand the wishes of the people with whose business they are entrusted.

But unless members of boards feel that they are entrusted by others with power to carry out what is a common interest, they cannot learn the lesson of political education which self-government is meant to teach. That lesson is one which many Governor-Generals and Governors of Provinces have tried to teach the people. Amongst those who have done much in this direction the names of Lord Mayo and the Marquis of Ripon stand foremost. The total income of these local boards exceeds 380 lakhs of rupees a year.

20. **The cities.** As a town grows in size the wealth and authority of its municipal board also increase. Accordingly it is in the capital cities of the provinces, rather than in the towns, that we find the citizens taking the largest part in governing themselves, and see how peace and commerce are the surest foundations upon which prosperity can be built. Since everyone ought to know the leading facts concerning the origin and growth of the capital cities of British India, a short account will now be given of the four great cities which are included in the 760 municipal towns mentioned above. They are Calcutta, the chief city of British India, capital of Bengal; Madras and Bombay, the capitals of the two presidencies bearing their names; and Rangoon, the capital of Burma. A short notice of the other capital cities of provinces will then complete the subject of this chapter.

21. **Calcutta.** At the close of the seventeenth century, as we shall see hereafter, Job Charnock, chief of the commercial business established by the British Company in Bengal, was allowed to settle on the banks of the Hugli in a small village. Charnock accordingly bought Calcutta and two neighbouring villages, and proceeded to fortify his factory against

CALCUTTA.

attack by land and river. In twenty years this petty village counted about 10,000 inhabitants. But it rapidly grew, and in 1750 had over 100,000. In 100 years more, *i.e.* by 1850, it had 400,000. The census of 1872 shewed 633,000, and now it has about 850,000. This is without its suburbs, which are really a part of the city. If these be included, Calcutta contains 1,106,000 inhabitants, and is one of the 12 largest cities in the world. A hundred years ago London, now the largest city in the world, with a population of over 4½ millions, or including its suburbs, of about 7 millions, was smaller than Calcutta now is.

Of the inhabitants of Calcutta, two-thirds are natives of other places, who come up to it for a time from the surrounding country to earn a livelihood, chiefly by working in the mills, or at some trade or industry. The prosperity of Calcutta has been due not only to the maintenance of public peace, but also to the triumph of skill and science over natural obstacles. The city is situated on the river Hugli, and is distant 80 miles from the sea. Ocean steamers have to come up this river, and about 50 years ago it was found that the silt or mud brought down by the Ganges from the hills was gradually filling up the channel of the river and making it shallower. Great alarm was felt, as it was feared that Calcutta would be quite cut off from the sea, and share the fate of many once flourishing seaport towns. But skilful engineers set to work. The silt is now dredged up from the bed of the river, and the channel is kept clean and open for the passage of steamers, and Calcutta still holds its own as the largest and most important port in India, with trade amounting to nearly 85 crores of rupees annually.

When the city had grown in numbers and in wealth, owing to trade and the preservation of peace, the British government offered, in 1840, to give over to the ratepayers the collection and management of the rates, if two-thirds of them, in any of the four quarters or districts into which the city was divided, should wish it. But they showed no such wish, and for several years different plans of making the city govern itself were tried and several public improvements were carried out.

In 1896 a corporation or council was formed with a chairman, vice-chairman and 75 commissioners, of whom two-thirds were elected by the ratepayers. A good deal of business was done, but it was found that there were too many members to do the work properly, for much time was wasted by them in talking. In 1899, the number of commissioners was fixed at 50, of whom half are elected by the ratepayers, ten are chosen by public bodies such as the Chamber of Commerce, the trades association and the Port Commissioners, and fifteen nominated by government. The chairman is paid a salary and is appointed by government, and may be removed on the request of not less than two-thirds of the commissioners. The ratepayers of the city do not even now take sufficient interest in self-government, as very few of them who are qualified to vote do so. This is to be regretted, because the income of the corporation is very large, amounting, in 1902-3, to more than 82 lakhs of rupees a year.

22. **Bombay** was given to the East India Company in 1668. Its revenue was then about Rs. 50,000, and its population consisted of about 10,000 "rogues and vagabonds." A hundred and fifty years later the residents were about 160,000. In less than 60 years from that date, in 1872, they had risen to 640,000, and despite heavy losses by plague they now number 982,000. Its growth from a collection of fishermen's huts, lying upon a sandy waste and

unhealthy swamp, to a stately city with splendid buildings and beautiful gardens, is marvellous. When the British first occupied it the air was so pestilential that seven governors died in 30 years, and no European child could live in it. Apart from the plague which has lately broken out, it is now a healthy city. The wonderful change which has taken place is due entirely to British protection. The ships which visited the western coast of India in times past were afraid to anchor in the splendid harbour of Bombay because of the pirates that infested the seas close by. Their forts and places of refuge were, however, completely destroyed in 1756.

In 1804 the Duke of Wellington, then Sir Arthur Wellesley, described the city as a place of refuge for the oppressed. "This island," he wrote, "has now become the only place of security in this part of India for property and for those who are objects of the Peshwa's enmity and vengeance, thus affording the strongest proof of the confidence which the natives repose in the justice and wisdom of our policy and our laws." The Peshwa, Baji rao, himself fled to Bombay when attacked by the great Maratha chief Holkar. The city was enlarged and the waters of the sea shut out by the construction of an embankment known as the Vellard in 1771. By these means Bombay, protected by sea and land, advanced rapidly in population and trade. During the wars in the Deccan and Guzerat, while the Maratha chiefs were fighting one another, a continuous stream of settlers sought protection under the British flag. Trade flourished in a harbour which

BOMBAY FROM THE TOP OF THE CLOCK TOWER.

gave splendid anchorage to ships, and was protected by the naval power of England. In 1802 the annual trade was less than a crore and a half of rupees. It is now worth 66 crores. The first cotton mill was erected in 1854, and to-day 400 factories, including cotton mills, are to be found in the city and presidency of Bombay.

In 1872, a town council and corporation were appointed and a system of election introduced. In 1888 certain changes were made, and there is now a corporation of 72 members called Commissioners, of whom 36 are elected by the ratepayers, 16 by the Justices of the Peace, 2 by the University and 2 by the Chamber of Commerce, and 16 are nominated by government. Any ratepayer may vote who pays rates amounting to Rs. 30 per annum. From among the members of the corporation a smaller body called the Town Council of 12 members are chosen, of whom 8 are elected by the other commissioners and 4 are nominated by government. The total income of the corporation was in 1902-03 more than 364 lakhs of rupees.

23. **Madras** has no harbour like that of Bombay, although in recent times stone piers have been run out into the sea so as to break the force of the waves and inclose smooth water within them, and thus form a port in which ships may lie at anchor, and land cargoes and passengers easily. In 1639 Mr. Francis Day, an officer of the East India Company who was looking about for a place on the east coast suitable for trade, succeeded in getting a small piece of land five miles along the coast by one mile in width inland,

on payment of a small rental. Here he built a fort, and invited traders of all kinds to come and settle close to it, to buy goods and to weave and sell cloth to the English merchants. During the wars between the English and French in India the fort was again and again besieged, and once taken by the French.

MADRAS.

Since the year 1758, however, it has enjoyed the priceless blessings of peace and safety. During troublous times, while the armies of Hyder devastated the Carnatic, rich bankers and wealthy traders came to live in Madras, to be safe under the guns of the fort, and the population and wealth of the town rapidly increased. The number of its inhabitants, which was about 400,000 in 1872, had risen to 450,000 in 1892, and is now a little over 500,000. Madras is a very healthy city to live in, as it is not nearly so crowded as Bombay and Calcutta. There are 29 persons per acre to 57 in Bombay and 68 in Calcutta. Fully two-thirds of the population are natives of the city. The system of election was applied to the municipal government in 1878. Various changes were made from time to time, as they were found to be necessary. In 1884 an Act was made by which 24 commissioners are elected by the ratepayers, and 10 nominated by government. Any ratepayer paying rates amounting to Rs. 25 per annum may vote for the election of a commissioner. The income of the municipality is about 24 lakhs.

24. **Rangoon**. This city, the capital of Burma, situated on the Irrawadi, was captured by the British in 1824, and afterwards restored to the king of Ava. It was again taken in April 1852, and finally annexed by the Marquis of Dalhousie, who predicted that it would become one of the greatest centres of trade in India, and used strong measures to suppress the pirates and robbers who infested the river and its banks. As soon as peace was established a peaceful population flocked to it, and in 1880 it was made a city, with large powers of self-government. The municipal area now contains 221,160 residents, and its affairs are managed by a board of 25 members, of whom only 3 are officials. Europeans, 13 in number, take an active part in its administration, and its income far exceeds that of Madras, amounting to sixty-five lakhs a year.

25. **Other capital cities.** The four cities just described are fortunate in being situated upon or near the open sea, to which ships carrying goods from and to foreign lands have easy access so long as peace is preserved by the armed forces of the King-Emperor. There is another great city, Karachi, capital of the province of Sindh, in the presidency of Bombay, which is also on the coast, and enjoys a trade as great as that of Madras. It has a population of 116,660 souls, and as it is the port of India nearest to Europe, it is sure to grow in wealth and importance. The city of Lucknow, the capital of Oudh, has 264,050 inhabitants; Lahore, the capital of the Punjab, has 203,000; and Allahabad, the capital of the United Provinces of Agra and Oudh, has more than 172,000. The last-mentioned province has several other great cities, including Benares, Cawnpore, Agra, and Meerut; while Nagpur, with 127,700 inhabitants, is the capital of the Central Provinces. Dacca, the new capital of the province of Eastern Bengal and Assam, has a smaller population of 91,000, but it is certain to attract a larger number of residents when its position is established. In all these, and many other smaller cities, municipal institutions exist, and the inhabitants of them enjoy not only security and peace, but the privileges of taking a part in their own government.

CHAPTER IV.

PROVINCES.

26. **Provinces**. Nine-tenths of the 294 millions who inhabit India live in villages and the remaining tenth in towns. The division of the population of the country into rural and urban, corresponds generally with their occupations, those who cultivate the land living in villages, and those who trade or work for manufacturers and merchants living in the towns. But for purposes of government or administration, some other division of the area and population is needed. The first step is to divide British India, which is directly ruled by the King-Emperor and his officials, from the Native States, which are under the administration of their own princes. British India is divided into 14 Provinces, which, as we shall see later on, are subdivided into districts, each of which includes a number of towns and villages. The names of villages and towns, as a rule, remain the same for ages, though changing rulers may alter the names and the extent of the provinces into which they divide countries. The fourteen provinces into which British India is now divided, are comparatively modern. In ancient times India included a great many kingdoms, each under its own ruler. Once in an age perhaps a powerful king like Asoka would conquer many countries, each of which would then be a province of his empire and be ruled by a governor under him. But sooner or later, after he had passed away, most, if not all of

these provinces would each of them become an independent kingdom under a ruler of its own. When the firm rule of Akbar had united all northern India into one great empire, provinces or subahs were formed, and each of them was again subdivided into sarkars or districts. Abul Fazl, one of the ministers of Akbar, tells us in the Ain-i-Akbari that the Moghal empire (about the year 1594) consisted of 105 sarkars and 2737 townships. The sarkars were grouped into 12 subahs, each of which was named after the ancient kingdom which it included or by its capital city. These subahs were Allahabad, Agra, Oudh, Ajmer, Ahmedabad, Behar, Bengal, Delhi, Kabul, Lahore, Multan, and Malwa. The number of subahs was afterwards raised to 15, when Berar, Khandesh and Ahmednagar were conquered. Each sarkar was subdivided into mahals.

27. **British provinces.** The 14 provinces of British India are called Madras, Bombay, Bengal, the United Provinces of Agra and Oudh, Punjab, the Central Provinces, to which is attached Berar, Eastern Bengal and Assam, Burma, Ajmer, Coorg, the North-West Frontier Province, British Baluchistan, and the Andamans. One can see at a glance that Akbar's India, which included Kabul, embracing Kashmir and Kandahar, extended further on the north-west. On the other hand, British India stretches far away to the east, right up to the river Mekong, embracing the whole of Burma, and on the south it covers nearly the whole map of India with possessions which had never submitted to that Emperor. And a great difference between Akbar's provinces and those of British India is that the latter,

with the exception of Berar which is held under a perpetual lease to the Government of India, do not include the native states. These were treated as a part of the Moghal empire while under Akbar's rule. Three-eighths of India are native states under native rulers, in alliance with the Supreme power.

28. **Government of the provinces.** It is very probable that from time to time the limits and size of some of the British Provinces may be altered. At present the provinces vary much in extent, three of them being under 3,200 square miles in area, while Bengal includes 110,054, and Burma 236,000 square miles. In population the difference between the provinces is still more striking. Each of them is under a ruler whose title varies from governor to lieutenant-governor or chief commissioner. Two of them, Madras and Bombay, are still called presidencies, and are under governors appointed in England, and aided by councils, over whom they preside. Five—Bengal, the United Provinces, Eastern Bengal and Assam, Punjab, and Burma—are under lieutenant-governors appointed by the Viceroy. In these seven provinces there are legislative councils, which will be described later on, for making laws and regulations. Each of them is allowed to keep for its own expenditure a large share of the money raised by taxation within its limits, called Provincial funds, the remainder being sent to the Supreme government to be spent on certain objects for the good of the whole of British India, and known as Imperial funds. Of the seven remaining provinces, the Central Provinces and Berar, which together make up an area of 100,396 square

miles, constitute one government larger in area, but less populous, than the Punjab, and are under a Chief Commissioner. The Andamans and Nicobars are a small civil administration of importance only because these islands are a settlement to which convicts from India are sent. These three provinces, for Berar is a province although under the same Government as the Central Provinces, are under the direct charge of the Government of India in the Home Department; while the four provinces known as the North-West Frontier province, Baluchistan, Ajmer, and Coorg, are administered by high political officers, also called Chief Commissioners, who are under the orders of the Government of India in the Political or Foreign Department.

29. **Madras.** The Madras Presidency is the oldest of the provinces. The first trading station in this province was established in 1611 at Masulipatam, which was abandoned in 1628 in favour of Armagaon, on the Coromandel coast; but the merchants returned to Masulipatam in 1632 by permission of the King of Golkonda. Francis Day was the founder of the Fort of St. George, built at a place called 'Chinapatam or Maderaspatam,' which was purchased from a raja of the country in 1639, and to this the Company's servants, or factors as they were called, at once removed their business. In 1653 Fort St. George was raised to the dignity of a Presidency, the head of the administration being called President.

Here the English merchants traded peaceably for a hundred years. In 1744 war broke out between the English and French, and the French leader, Dupleix, attempted to drive the English traders out of Southern India so that the French might have all the trade to themselves. The French took Madras, but when the news reached England, English soldiers and an English fleet came out, retook their own town and went on to capture Pondicherry, the chief French trading station. A few years afterwards, in 1760, they took Masulipatam and the Northern Sarkars, a strip of country on the east coast, north of Madras, which at that time belonged to the French. The Emperor of Delhi, Shah Alam, then the Overlord of the country, made a grant of the northern Sarkars to Colonel Clive, the English leader, in 1764. This strip of country, with the town of Madras, was the beginning of the Madras Presidency.

How Hyder Ali, a soldier of fortune, took Mysore from the ancient Hindu dynasty, which had ruled the country for centuries, how he attacked the allies of the English, and how war arose between the English and Hyder and his son Tippu Sultan, may be learnt from Indian history. In the end the English were victorious, and in 1793 Malabar, on the western coast, and the districts in the Carnatic, now called Salem, were ceded to Lord Cornwallis by Tippu; while in 1799 three other districts were, on the defeat and death of Tippu, added to British territory, and Mysore was restored to its ancient Hindu rule. About the same time, in 1799, Bellary and Cuddapa were ceded by the Nizam of Hyderabad. In 1801 the Nawab of the Carnatic, who had conspired against the English, with whom he was in alliance, to help Tippu, died, leaving no son, and the rest of the Carnatic lapsed to the Company. In 1838 the small district of

LORD CLIVE.

From an engraving by Bartolozzi, after the picture by Nathaniel Dance.

Kurnool was annexed. Thus it will be seen that in about 50 years the small trading station of Madras grew into a great province. It has now an area of about 142,000 square miles and 38 millions of people.

30. **Bombay.** Only 26 years before British traders bought Madras from the Hindu raja, a British factory had been established on the western coast at Surat under a grant from Jehangir, emperor of Delhi, to Sir Thomas Roe, an ambassador to the Moghal court from James I., king of England. The next year, 1614, the Emperor issued orders allowing the merchants of King James the privileges of free trade throughout his empire. In 1668 Bombay with its fine harbour was acquired not from any native chief, but by its transfer to the East India Company on a small payment from the King of England, to whom the Portuguese had ceded it in 1661, as part of the dowry of the Spanish Princess, who married Charles II. The headquarters of the Company's trade on the west coast of India were moved from Surat to that island, and in 1708 the settlement was made a Presidency. Here the English merchants traded in peace for the next 60 years. In 1775 Raghunath rao, better known as Raghuba, the Peshwa of the Marathas,

SIR THOMAS ROE.

who was opposed by the other Maratha chiefs, asked the Bombay government to help him, and gave them the two islands of Salsette and Bassein, which are close to Bombay, as the price of their help. A war followed, and in the end peace was made, and by the Treaty of Salbai in 1782 the other Maratha chiefs agreed that the Company should keep these islands. Twenty years later Baji rao, the son of Raghuba, who was then Peshwa, was attacked by Holkar, a powerful Maratha chief, and fled to Bombay to save his life. By this time the British had become the greatest power in the country, and Lord Wellesley, who was then Governor-General, saw that the only way in which peace could be secured throughout the vast continent of India was to establish one strong central government, which should be acknowledged by all other kings and rulers; keep them from fighting with one another; and make them rule their own territories properly. Baji rao agreed to this by the treaty of Bassein in 1802. To pay for the cost of the war, which had to be waged with the other Maratha chiefs who refused to agree, he ceded to the Company some of the districts which now form part of the Presidency. After the battle of Kirkee in 1817 the Deccan (excluding Hyderabad) and the Konkan were added to the Presidency in 1817. Sindh was annexed in 1843 and included in it. The Bombay Presidency has enjoyed peace for the last 85 years. Its population is now about 18½ millions, and its area about 123,000 square miles.

31. **Bengal.** The growth of Bengal was due to the same causes which led to that of Madras and Bombay, but it was more marked and more rapid.

The Emperor Shah Jehan permitted the East India Company to set up a factory at Hugli, near the mouth of the Ganges, in 1640, the year after they acquired Madras. In 1681 Bengal was separated from Madras, and a governor, Mr. Hedges, was appointed to take charge of the various factories at Patna, Balasor, Dacca, and other places in that part of India. But the Moghal governor of Bengal treated the British merchants with great severity, and Job Charnock retired from Hugli in 1686 to Chatanati. This village and two others called Govindpur and Kalikata, were purchased from Prince Azim Ushan in 1698, and, on the site of the last, Fort William was built. Kalikata, or Calcutta, became a Presidency in 1707, and for the next fifty years the Company carried on their trade in peace. But on the 20th of June, 1756, Siraj-ad-daula attacked Fort William and thrust its occupants, 146 Englishmen, into the *Black Hole*, where all save 23 died in a single night. War followed, and in 1765 the Moghal Emperor, Shah Alam, conferred upon the Company the diwani of Bengal, Behar, and Orissa. In 1803, Orissa was taken from the Marathas, who had seized upon it, and the whole province of Bengal, which then included part of the present United Provinces, was placed under a governor. In 1834 the governor of Bengal was made Governor-General of India. He continued to govern the province of Bengal, without a Council, till 1854, in which year the first Lieutenant-Governor of Bengal was appointed. In the meantime, in 1836, the Upper Provinces had been detached, and included in what were then called the North-West Provinces. In 1874 it was found that Bengal was too large for one province, and Assam was made into a separate government. Again, in 1905, the size of Bengal was reduced by transferring three divisions, Dacca, Chittagong, and Rajshahi, with the district of Malda, to a new province which included Assam; but Bengal still counts a population of 50,723,000 and an area of 110,054 square miles.

32. **The United Provinces of Agra and Oudh.** This province was, until 1902, known as the North-West Province, because, when it was so called, it formed the north-west limit of British India. When Bengal was ceded to the British, its population grew rapidly rich and prosperous under their rule. But in the country beyond there were civil wars and anarchy. The Afghans and Marathas ravaged it in turn. The English Company had given all the help it could to Shuja daula, nawab of Oudh, in the hope that as a strong and friendly power, he would prove a good neighbour and protect his own and their territory from attack. But this he failed to do. During the wars with the Marathas, the territory of the Doab which lies between the Jumna and Ganges, was given up to the British by the Maratha chief Sindhia, after his defeats at Assaye and Laswaree in 1805. This formed the province of Agra. British authority was extended up to the Sutlej in 1808, and the Sagar and Narbada territories, afterwards incorporated in the Central Provinces, were ceded by the raja of Nagpur in 1811. The hill tracts of Kamaon and Garhwal and Dehradun were added after the Gurkha war in 1816.

The kingdom of Oudh, in which tyranny, oppression and misgovernment had been carried to their utmost limit, was taken from the Nawab after repeated warnings in 1856, and in 1877 united with the North-West Provinces. On the formation of a new North-West Frontier province, on the north-west of the Punjab in 1901, the name was changed to that of the United Provinces of Agra and Oudh. The Lieutenant-Governor has his headquarters at Allahabad. The population is 47½ millions, and the area about 107,000 square miles.

33. **The Punjab**. The province of Punjab, watered by the five rivers—the Sutlej, Beas, Ravi, Chenab and Jhelum—was created almost at a single step like that of Bengal. It was not slowly built up, like the United Provinces, after many wars, but the whole of it fell into the hands of the British owing to causes which are easily explained.

The East India Company wished to leave the country beyond the Sutlej outside their dominion, and therefore in 1809 made a treaty with Ranjit Singh which gave him leave to assert his own authority over the province. This he did by suppressing all the native states and keeping up a powerful army. On his death, in 1839, his successors failed to keep the soldiers in order, and the army, numbering 72,000 men, with 381 guns, created disturbances. British territory was invaded, and the authorities, forced to protect their north-western province, defeated the Sikh army, and took possession of a part of the Lahore state, leaving the remaining districts to be administered for the future Maharaja, then a child. This act of self-denial was not understood, and when, in 1848, two British officers were murdered at

Multan, the Sikh army again came to blows with the British. After suffering four defeats they laid down their arms, and Lord Dalhousie saw no other course but to annex the Lahore state and provide a pension for the Maharaja and his family. The province was first governed by a board of three members, and then, in 1853, by a chief commissioner. In 1859 it was placed under a Lieutenant-Governor. Its chief city is Lahore, and the population is now over 20 millions. The area is about 97,000 square miles.

LORD DUFFERIN.

34. **Burma.** In the year 1826, Aracan, Tavoy, and Tennaserim were taken from the king of Burma, who without any provocation had invaded British India. There was a second war in 1852, which ended in the annexation of Pegu by Lord Dalhousie, and in 1885 a third war resulted in the conquest of Upper Burma, when Lord Dufferin was Viceroy. In 1862 the lower provinces had been placed under a Chief Commissioner, and in 1897 both Upper and Lower Burma were united under a Lieutenant-Governor, whose

headquarters are at Rangoon. The area of the province, which is the largest in India, is 236,700 square miles. It includes 36 districts with a population of 10½ millions. As the country was filled with disorder which desolated the villages and reduced the population during the rule of the Avan kings, it is certain that now that there are peace and order and good government, its population will greatly increase. In the 10 years from 1892 to 1902 it had risen from 7½ to 10½ millions. The port of Rangoon, protected by the British navy, has become one of the largest centres of trade and commerce in the empire.

35. **The Central Provinces and Berar**. These provinces include territories conquered from Sindhia and the Raja of Nagpur in 1818, and the rest of the native state of Nagpur, which was annexed in 1853, when the raja died without an heir. In 1862, Sambalpur and some other districts were taken out of the Province of Bengal, and at a later date, in consequence of various exchanges of territory between the British government and certain native states, Nimar was also added. In this way one united province, called the Central Provinces, was formed and placed under a Chief Commissioner in 1861. The Province has lately restored the greater part of Sambalpur to Bengal, but it still retains a population of nearly 12 millions, and an area, including Berar, of 100,396 square miles. The capital town is Nagpur. Quite lately the country of Berar, with a population of 2¾ millions and an area of close on 18,000 square miles, which belongs to the Nizam of Hyderabad, and was, in 1854,

assigned to the Company for the payment of a military force, has been put under the government of the Central Provinces, being leased to the British government under an arrangement concluded by Lord Curzon. Berar, which ranks as a province, is thus a portion of the native state of Hyderabad, but since the lease of it is perpetual, its administration rests entirely with the Government of India, and is similar in all important respects to that of the Central Provinces.

36. **Eastern Bengal and Assam.** Assam was made a province in 1874, by separating from Bengal two districts, Sylhet and Goalpara, which had formed part of it when it was ceded to the British as a part of Bengal by the Emperor of Delhi in 1765. To them were added other districts, including that of Assam, from which the province took its first name, which were conquered from the Burmese in 1826. Other portions of the hill districts were added from time to time, as they were annexed to punish the wild and lawless hill tribes which inhabited them when they attacked villages within British territory. In 1905 the increasing amount of business devolving upon the Lieutenant-Governor of Bengal led to the detachment of nine districts from Eastern Bengal and eight more from Northern Bengal, which were added to the thirteen districts of Assam and placed under a Lieutenant-Governor with his capital at Dacca. The province of Eastern Bengal and Assam now includes 101,147 square miles with a population of 30¾ millions of whom eighteen millions are Muhammadans.

37. **The North-West Frontier Province**, with an area of 16,400 square miles and a population of over two millions, has been very recently formed to the north-west of the Punjab. It includes the districts of the Punjab to the west of the Indus, with its capital at Peshāwar. The head of the province is styled Agent to the Governor-General.

38. **Ajmer-Merwara.** This province is in Rajputana. Ajmer was received from Sindhia, in 1818, in exchange for certain territories which had been acquired from the Peshwa. Merwara fell to the Company as its share of a district rescued from gangs of plunderers by a British force sent to assist the Rajput states of Mewar and Marwar. The Resident in Rajputana is also Chief Commissioner of the province which measures 2700 square miles and has a population of nearly half a million.

39. **Coorg** is a small province in the Western Ghats on the west of Mysore. Its area is about 1600 square miles and its population 181,000. Its raja, Vira Rajendra Wodiar, treated the people so cruelly that numbers of them fled to British territory for protection. As the raja refused to listen to advice or amend his ways, he was in 1834 deposed by a British force. The headmen of Coorg then held a darbar, and requested that the British would annex the country, which was done. The capital of Coorg is Mercara and the Resident in Mysore is the Chief Commissioner.

40. **British Baluchistan**, with an area of about 46,000 square miles and a population of 308,000, is a part of the empire on the south of Afghanistan,

and is governed by a Chief Commissioner whose headquarters are at Quetta. The district of Quetta came under British rule in 1879, the Bori valley in 1884 and the Zhob district in 1889.

41. **The Andamans**, with Port Blair as their capital, were made the penal settlement for Indian convicts in 1858. They form a chain of four principal and several smaller islands in the Indian Ocean, distant 450 miles from Rangoon. The Nicobar Islands are close to them, and the total area of all of them is 3000 square miles, and the population about 25,000.

CHAPTER V.

THE NATIVE STATES.

42. **Foreign territory**. If you look at a map of India, you will see that there are large tracts of country not included in the 14 provinces of British India that have been described. They are called Native States. All of them taken together make up an area more than half as large as British India. There are altogether nearly 700 of these states, some of them very large and others including only a few villages. But in one point they are all alike. Although they are all parts of the continent of India and of the British empire in India, yet they are not parts of the territory under British law and known as British India. They are not ruled by officers of the King-Emperor, although they are

protected by his Majesty, who is their Overlord. They have their own laws and their own courts of justice. The people who live in them are directly subjects of their chiefs, and, in short, the states are not British but foreign territory.

But although these states are not directly under our government, yet they are situated in India, of which they form a part, and it makes a great difference to us whether they are well or ill governed. If civil war should break out in one of the larger states, or if the government should be overturned and the country overrun by bands of robbers, it would be very hard to keep them out of British territory. This is just what caused the Pindari war, as we know from history. If a native army should refuse to obey the ruler of the state or its own officers, as the armies of Gwalior and of the Punjab once did, our own country might be invaded, as it then was, and a cruel and costly war would be the result. Or if a powerful ruler were to make a treaty with our enemies, as Tippu Sultan once did with the French, we might have to fight both by land and sea. The native ruler and his state might be ruined, and we should be put to great loss and many of our soldiers killed. And if the chiefs who rule in the smaller states should shelter gangs of robbers or encourage evil customs like suttee or infanticide, which are forbidden in the neighbouring British villages, the people who live in the latter might be tempted to follow their bad example, and the difficulty of putting a stop to evil practices would be increased. It is therefore for the good of the inhabitants of British India and of the native states themselves that they should be well governed.

43. **A difficult task.** It was no easy matter to preserve so many states in the Indian Empire, and success was not attained without some failures and several changes of policy. Before British rule, all the weaker states were sooner or later annexed by a stronger power as by the Moghal Emperor of Delhi or Ranjit Singh of the Punjab. But except, perhaps, the great Akbar and his immediate successors, there never has been, in times within our knowledge, any power so much stronger than all the rest as to take the place of Overlord or Supreme Sovereign of India, maintain peace and order throughout the country, and at the same time preserve the weaker and smaller states. The best way of doing this was only found out after a long time, after repeated trials and experiments. In the old days it seemed to British rulers as if the only way to preserve a weak state from ruin was to annex it. Even after the success of the wars which the East India Company had been compelled to wage in defence of its own factories, and after the Company had become the strongest of the great powers of India, the difficulty of converting the princes and chiefs of neighbouring states into friends and allies was so great as to seem a hopeless task.

44. **Policy of non-interference.** At first it was thought that if the rulers of the states were left alone, and no alliances made with them, they in turn might leave the British merchants to pursue their trade in peace and quiet. The East India Company, which had obtained leave from the Moghal Emperor to trade

and had then proceeded, peaceably and lawfully, to establish their factories on the sea-shore, had no wish to rule over extensive territories. Their object was to engage in profitable commerce, not to take part in wars and intrigues. When their traders and servants had to defend themselves, and to fight as the only way to escape from being driven into the sea, and when, as a consequence of the wars thus forced upon them, the Company began to obtain countries by conquest or treaty, the British Parliament did all it could to keep them from acquiring fresh dominion. Accordingly, in the reign of George III., An Act of Parliament, passed in 1793, declared that "To pursue schemes of conquest and extension of dominion are measures repugnant to the wish, the honour, and the policy of this nation."

LORD WELLESLEY.

The Company in England tried to carry out this view, and in their letters, many of which have been published by order of Parliament, they again and again forbade their officers in India to enter into any engagements with native states that could be avoided, or meddle with any native prince. They said that they wished their governors and other servants to abstain from all interference in matters which did not concern them. This policy or plan of letting things alone was known as the "non-intervention" or "let alone" policy. But the consequence was that outside the British territories there were wars all over India. Many states in Central India and Rajputana were becoming deserts. The country was going fast to ruin. Disorder prevailed everywhere.

45. **Subsidiary alliances.** The first British statesman to perceive what ought to be done to preserve peace throughout India was Lord Wellesley. When he came out to India in 1798, he found that Tippu Sultan of Mysore had been writing to the French, then the deadly foes of the British, asking them to help him to drive them out of India, and he knew other native powers were in league with him. At the same time the Nizam of Hyderabad, whom the British government was bound by treaty to assist, was attacked by powerful enemies and was in great danger. It was clear to Lord Wellesley that matters would get worse and worse, and that wars would never cease if the native princes were allowed to do as they pleased, and that in the end the British would have to fight to defend themselves or make up their minds to leave the country altogether. He determined to make the British, who were at that time the strongest and the most civilised of the great powers of India, supreme throughout the country, undertaking the general responsibility of protecting one and all from foreign invasion, of defending

each of the smaller states from its enemies, and of maintaining peace and order everywhere.

It would be necessary that each of these states should contribute a share, smaller or larger according to its size, to the cost of the great standing army which protected it. As this contribution was called a subsidy, and the force which protected each of the larger states a subsidiary force, Lord Wellesley's system is known as the subsidiary system. That this system should succeed, it was needful that each and every state should agree to it, and if any state would not agree, it was needful to use force to make it do so. Tippu refused, and was crushed. The Nizam agreed gladly, for to him it meant safety and peace. His successor, the firm friend and ally of the British, still rules Hyderabad, the greatest Muhammadan state in India. The Gaekwar also agreed, and one of his descendants still rules Baroda as an ally of the British. Of the other great powers some agreed at first, but they afterwards changed their minds, and made war.

46. **A return to the "Let alone" policy.** Lord Wellesley did not stay long enough in India to complete his work. And the East India Company found that the wars which he had made cost a great deal of money, and took away all the profits of trade. The British Parliament and many great men in England did not approve of what he had done. They had never been in India, and had not seen for themselves the state of affairs there, as Lord Wellesley had. If they had supported him and carried out his policy fully, there would speedily have

been peace everywhere, and the enormous increase of trade and of cultivation that would have followed, besides the cessation of expenditure on war, would have scon raised the profits of the merchants beyond any point they had reached before. There was, no doubt, a great increase of expenditure necessary at first, and this was all they looked at. They did not allow time for the effect of the subsidiary system to be seen. Accordingly Lord Cornwallis, who had previously served as Governor-General and avoided as far as possible making any alliances with the states, returned to Calcutta, with orders to go back to the "let alone" policy and to meddle no more with any Indian prince.

47. **A general protectorate.** This policy of leaving the chiefs of native territories without the protection and control of the British power was followed for the next ten years, and the effect of it was by that time clearly seen. All Central India was again filled with disorder. Armies of robbers, called Pindaris, roamed all over the country. The Rajput chiefs, who had been in alliance with the British and depended on them for help and protection, were attacked by their enemies. The Gurkhas invaded British India on the north. The great Maratha chiefs, headed by the Peshwa, attacked the British troops in their country. The Marquis of Hastings, who had come out as Governor-General in 1813, saw how matters stood, and informed the British government and the Company at home that the only way to save the country was to return to Lord Wellesley's policy, and this he was allowed to do. After five years of

constant warfare he succeeded in bringing all India, except the Punjab, under British protection. His purpose was to manage for the native chiefs all matters that concerned their relations and dealings with other powers and chiefs, leaving them to govern their own subjects inside their dominions as they might please.

48. **Misrule and annexation.** Wars had now ceased between the native princes and between them and the British. There was peace throughout India, and this in itself was a priceless boon to the people. But the work of securing to the subjects of native states comfort, safety and good government was only half done. The condition of affairs was bad for all parties. The rulers knew that the British would preserve their states, and they had been told that they might manage their own affairs as they pleased. On the other hand, their subjects were no longer able to invite a neighbouring chief to help them in getting rid of a tyrant, and if they rose against their ruler in rebellion the British authorities were certain to interfere if disorder spread beyond the limits of the state. Some chiefs, as for instance in Coorg, Tanjore, and Oudh, took advantage of this state of affairs, and their oppressed subjects called upon the Company to help them. What then was to be done by the Supreme Power, which had undertaken to have no concern with the administration of the protected chiefs, and at the same time was bound to maintain order and put down disturbances in the Indian Empire?

The only effective remedy that at that time

suggested itself to the Supreme Power was to annex any state if the inhabitants desired it or if its ruler utterly misgoverned it. The people of Coorg in this way asked that they might become the subjects of the Queen-Empress Victoria, and their wish was granted. In other cases states were annexed when their rulers died leaving no direct male heir, and when according to rule they could not adopt a successor without first obtaining the permission of the overlord, the British government. In private life, when a rich man dies without heirs his property 'lapses' to the Crown, that is to say, it is taken over by the government, and if no heir ever appears, it is used for the general good of the people. In the same way, it was at that time thought that the best arrangement would be that the state should be taken over and ruled by the British government to which it was said to have 'lapsed.' In the time of Lord Dalhousie several Hindu states, such as Satara, Jaitpur, Jhansi, and Nagpur, were thus annexed, liberal allowances being granted to the families of the last chief and the right of adoption being refused. This policy, however, was very unpopular, and instead of annexing a state as a cure for misrule, it was thought better to prevent misrule by interfering, when the need arose, in the interests of its oppressed subjects.

49. **Adoptions allowed.** Accordingly, after the retirement of Lord Dalhousie, the right of adoption was conferred upon all important rulers of native states, and, as a consequence, steps were taken to interfere promptly whenever a chief followed oppressive and

bad courses of government. This new policy was introduced in 1858, when the government of India was transferred to the Crown and Queen Victoria became the Ruler of India. Her Majesty's proclamation to the Indian people, including the princes of the native states, is given in full in the last chapter of this book. It is justly regarded as the 'Magna Charta' of India, the great charter or document which secures for ever to the people of India their rights and liberties. The chiefs are assured that as long as they are loyal to the Crown and faithful to their engagements, they will be protected and their states perpetuated. So long as they act so, they need fear no annexation to British dominion.

Such advice as may be needed is given to a ruling chief by an experienced British officer, styled a Resident, or by a political officer of lower rank, who resides at his capital to help him. If any chief is proved to be unfit to rule, he may be deposed, but the state is not annexed. Another chief, usually his nearest qualified relative, is appointed chief in his stead. And a prince who has no heir is allowed to adopt one, so that his state cannot lapse. In order that young princes may be qualified to rule, when their turn comes, they are very carefully educated, either by a private tutor or at a 'chief's college,' where the education is the best that can be secured, and where the young princes are not only given such knowledge as can be acquired from books, but are instructed in manly exercises, such as cricket, polo, shooting, and fencing.

50. **Classes of states.** The states protected by the government of India may be divided into three

classes: firstly, those which lie close to one another and form large blocks of territory subject to native rule; secondly, states of large area each of which is surrounded by British territory; and thirdly, small scattered principalities which lie inside British districts or provinces. Of the first class, the Rajputana Agency, the Central India Agency, Baluchistan and Kathiawar are the most important. Of the second class, Kashmir, Hyderabad, Mysore, and Baroda are the chief, but Travancore, Kolhapur, and Kutch may also be mentioned as considerable states. In the third class are included some hundreds of states which vary in size from that of a district to a small group of villages.

A RAJA OF RAJPUTANA.

51. **Rajputana**. The Rajputana Agency covers an area of about 128,000 square miles and is therefore larger than the whole of Bombay and Sind. It has a population of nearly 10 millions. It includes twenty states, of which Tonk is Muhammadan, Bharatpur and Dholpur are Jat, and the rest Rajput. In the extensive deserts of Rajputana the Rajputs, driven out of Hindustan by the Muhammadans, found a refuge for hundreds of years, and thus their chiefs of Mewar or Udaipur, Marwar or Jodhpur, and Jaipur

rank as the oldest princely families in India. Among the other states may be mentioned Bikaner, Bundi, Karauli, Bharatpur, Alwar, Kota, and Banswara. They had suffered in turn from the exactions of the Delhi emperors, from the incursions of the Pindaris and the attacks and invasions of the Marathas, when in 1818 they were brought under the protection of the British. The chief political officer resides at Abu and is styled Agent to the Governor-General.

52. **Central India Agency.** This Agency includes 148 states, ten of them ruled by chiefs who are entitled to the honour of salutes, which make up a solid block of nearly 79,000 square miles in the very heart of India, with a population of nearly 9 millions. Both in size and in the number of its inhabitants it somewhat resembles the British province known as the Central Provinces. Gwalior, a Maratha state, containing an area of 25,000 square miles and 3,000,000 inhabitants, ruled by the Sindhia family, Bhopal governed by a Muhammadan family of Afghan descent, and Indore, ruled by the Holkars, are the chief states, while Rewa, Orcha, Datia, and Dhar come next. The chief political officer resides at Indore, from which centre he exercises control over the whole Agency.

53. **Baluchistan.** Baluchistan lies beyond the plains of the Indus, on the western frontier of India, and guards the approaches into Hindustan from Persia and Afghanistan. It consists of the territories of the Khan of Kelat, with an area of 72,000 square miles, and the Jam of Las Beyla. Together with the British province of Quetta, or British Baluchistan, it is under

the political control of an officer of the government of India who resides at Quetta. The country includes a large tract of desert with a population of less than half a million, excluding the residents in Kharan and Makran, which are under British administration.

54. **Kathiawar**. The only other large block of chiefships which needs notice is that of Kathiawar, a peninsula containing 20,560 square miles with several fair ports on the west of India and included in the presidency of Bombay. It is a good instance of the efforts made by the British government to save native states from annexation. Under its treaty with the Peshwa the East India Company might have made Kathiawar a British province, but it preferred to take the chiefs under its protection rather than under its direct rule. To the numerous chiefs the British government has given jurisdiction and authority in various degrees or classes, and cases, whether civil or criminal, which lie beyond the jurisdiction of any petty chief are decided for him by political officers under an agent at Rajkote.

NIZAM-UL-MULK.

55. **Hyderabad.** Hyderabad, with an area of about 83,000 square miles and a population of about 11 millions, is nearly as large as the Agra portion of the United Provinces. Its founder, the first Nizam, was a servant of the emperor of Delhi, who about two hundred years ago shook off the authority of his master when the Muhammadan power began to decline. His successors have received several large additions of territory from the British government as a reward for their services.

56. **Kashmir.** Kashmir, including Jammu, with an area of about 81,000 square miles and a population of close on 3 millions, is about as large as Hyderabad. It was created by the British after the defeat of the Sikh army at the battle of Sobraon in 1846. The hill country between the rivers Indus and Ravi, then acquired by conquest, was conferred upon Gulab Singh, raja of Jammu, by the treaty of Amritsar.

57. **Mysore.** Mysore, a large state in South India, covering nearly 30,000 square miles, with a population of 5½ millions, rich in gold and fertile in soil, also owes its existence to the British, by whom it was restored, in 1799, to the Hindu dynasty from whom it had been taken by Hyder. Some years afterwards, the people of Mysore rose against the oppressions and exactions of their Maharaja, and the British government were obliged to depose him and administer the government for a time. At first they decided to annex the state as its last ruler had no son of his own, but in the end they allowed him to adopt a son, who was educated by an English tutor and granted ruling powers in 1881. The government

was thus restored to native rule after it had been conducted by British officers for fifty years. The young Maharaja, who ruled his country well, died after a short reign and was succeeded by his son, the present Maharaja, in 1894. He was then, however, a minor, and the government was conducted by his mother as Maharani Regent, with the help of a Diwan, till 1902, when the young chief was placed in power. He too has been very carefully educated, and the country is well governed and prosperous.

58. **Baroda.** Baroda is a small but very rich state with an area of 8000 square miles and a population of about 2 millions. It stands by itself in the fertile division of Guzerat in Western India. A Maratha chief named Damaji founded the line of Gaekwars who still rule this state, which was preserved by the British from absorption in the Peshwa's dominion, and protected from other encroachments while the British factories at Surat and Bombay were themselves in difficulties. More recently, on the deposition, for misconduct, of its ruler in 1875, the British government allowed the widow of a former Gaekwar to adopt a member of the ruling family who had been selected by the government of India as a suitable person to rule the country.

59. **Other states.** Besides the four states just described Nepal, with an area of 54,000 square miles, has a British Resident who is directly under the government of India, which also controls the agents in Rajputana, Central India, and Baluchistan. Under the government of Madras there are five, under Bombay 354, under the United Provinces

two, and under Bengal and Burma 34 and 53 states respectively. The chief commissioner of the Central Provinces and the Lieutenant Governor of Eastern Bengal and Assam deal with a few petty states in their neighbourhood. Many of these states are small, and some are little more than estates. In the Bombay province petty states are mixed up with British districts, so that the main roads pass in and out of British and foreign territory. The honour of a salute, which varies from twenty-one guns to nine, shows in a general way the rank held by a native chief. To the rulers of the three states of Baroda, Hyderabad, and Mysore the highest salute is given, and to the chiefs of eight states, Bhopal, Gwalior, Indore, Kashmir, Kelat, Kolhapur, Mewar, and Travancore, salutes of nineteen guns are granted. Thirteen chiefs are entitled to seventeen guns, and seventeen receive a salute of fifteen guns. Besides these, there are sixty-five other chiefs who are honoured with salutes. Judged, then, by this standard, there are in India one hundred and six rulers of states who stand in the front rank. These figures, however, include several of the states which are massed together in groups, like the Rajput and Central India states, as well as those which lie apart from others.

Amongst the chief estates which rank as native states may be mentioned the Jágirs of Satara and the Southern Maratha country, the chiefships of the Central Provinces and those of Orissa. It is not necessary to give a list of them, but any one who looks at the map of India will see at a glance that if these states should prove bad neighbours, or unable to maintain peace and order, they would cause very great trouble and anxiety to the government of the province in which they are situated, and to the officers of the British districts close to them. A weak central government would long ago have given up as hopeless the task of controlling so many chiefships without the aid of British law and British courts. Their preservation is honourable both to the chiefs themselves and to the British government. It shows that the Supreme government is strong enough to protect the rights of the weak, and it also shows the good sense of those chiefs who accept advice and work by the side of the British officer for the good of the people.

60. **Advantages of native rule.** The British government gains several advantages by the continuance of native rule. Each state is a standing proof of the faithfulness with which the government of India keeps the promises made in the Queen's proclamation. The native states also enable the people of India to compare the results of various systems of government. Those who wish to find out whether population, education, commerce and industry increase more rapidly, and whether a country prospers better under one form of government than under another, may answer this question by observing the results in British India and in the native states. And if any one living in British India thinks that native rule is better than British, he may go over to a native state and live there, if he likes. The rulers of the states relieve the British authorities of

the task of governing a large part of the empire, and their loyalty and goodwill are of high value to the protecting power. On the other hand, the British government probably gives more to the states than they contribute to the welfare of the empire. The cost of the navy and army which defend the empire, the upkeep of the ports and dockyards, the greater part of the expenditure on railroads, and the expense of the postal and telegraph and other imperial departments which benefit the whole of India, are borne almost entirely by the British provinces. But, at the same time, the princes and chiefs relieve the British government of heavy responsibilities and some expense, and to a certain extent their subjects indirectly pay duties on articles brought into British ports. All observers say that under British advice great improvements have been made in the mode of government of the states, and all friends of India trust that the rulers of the native states and of the countries in British India will try to do their best, and endeavour to make the people under their government prosperous and happy. It is to be hoped that the methods and rules of civilised government, which the British have brought to India from Europe, will be taken up and adapted by native rulers to the customs and the feelings of their own subjects.

CHAPTER VI.

THE DISTRICT.

61. **Districts**. Although the native states are part of the Indian empire and their inhabitants owe allegiance to the King-Emperor and must keep the peace, yet there are many duties and privileges of a citizen which only concern the people of British India. We must therefore go back to the provinces and learn some more details about them. British India is divided into provinces, as we have seen, and these provinces are, for purposes of government, again divided into districts, of which there are altogether 259, including those of Berar which are held under a perpetual lease to the government of India. The names of many of these districts are the same now as they were ages ago, although their size and boundaries may have been altered, just as the names of most Indian villages have remained unchanged for thousands of years. In the old times many of the modern districts were known as countries, ruled each by its own raja or nawab. Under Akbar the subahs or provinces were divided into sarkars or zillas, to which the districts of our time more or less correspond. A province is a group of districts, and each district is complete in itself. The government of one district is very much like that of another—that is to say, it has very much the same set of government officers, who follow the same rules and are guided by the same laws, so that if we know

all about the administration or government of one district we have a very fair acquaintance with that of all the rest. If we were to go to a district in the north of India we should meet with officials of the same character as those we see in the south, and the way in which they do their work would be very much the same.

As citizens of the empire we ought to study very carefully the administration of a district. By doing this we learn how the whole empire is governed, for the empire is merely a collection of native states governed under one system, and 259 districts administered under another according to British laws. If any one of these districts is well governed, then we may conclude that the whole empire is well governed. For, as the administration of all the districts is very much the same, if it should be found that the present system of governing one district works well, then we may believe that on the whole the administration of the empire works well. At the same time there are as many and as great differences in the character and social customs of the people as there are in the nature of the soil, the climate, and the rainfall of the various provinces, and these require different treatment. Accordingly districts vary much in size and population, and there are even special and local laws which apply to one class of the people or to one tract of country and not to another. But the general principles and plan of British government are the same everywhere, and it is fairly correct to say that each district is a test of the government of the empire, a standard by which we may judge of the government of British India.

62. **Districts parts of the province.** A district being one part of a large province cannot be considered by the ruler of the province without thought of the rest of the country under his charge. The father of a large family cannot think only of one child. He must do his best for all his children. If one child be weak and sickly, he may have to spend a great deal more upon it than upon the other children who are strong and healthy. The ruler of a province must do what is best for the province as a whole. If one of his districts is poor, barren and backward, or if in another there should be some natural calamity, such as a famine or flood, he may have to spend more money on it in irrigation or railways or famine relief or in other ways than on other districts which are rich and fertile and have more natural advantages. The money raised by taxation in the poor district may be much less than that collected in rich districts, but the latter ought not to complain if the ruler of the province should spend a part of the money raised in them on the former. It is important for citizens to remember this, because it is natural for us to think first of ourselves and to claim as much as we can of the revenues of the state. Our rulers, however, must take a wider view of their responsibilities.

63. **Area of the district.** In dividing a country into counties or districts, a good ruler will try to give to each district officer more or less equal work to do. The Indian districts, however, vary much in size and population in the different provinces. Taking all the

259 districts together, and excluding the four capital cities of Calcutta, Bombay, Madras and Rangoon, their average size is about 4000 square miles, and their average population about 900,000. But in some provinces the districts are much larger and in others smaller. Thus the average size of a district in Madras is nearly 6000, in Bengal a little over 3000, and in the United Provinces a little over 2000 square miles. The smallest district in India is Simla, with an area of 101 square miles, and the largest Upper-Chindwin, in Upper Burma, with an area of 19,000 square miles. If we look at the population we find that an average district in Madras has about 1½ millions of inhabitants, in Bengal also about 1½ millions, and in the United Provinces about a million.

How is it that some districts are so much larger than others, and why do some contain a much greater population than others? The answer is that the work is much heavier in some of the smaller districts. And although the work of the ruler or collector of a district mainly depends upon the size of his district and upon its population, it is also affected by other things. He cannot manage a district of more than a certain size, for he has not only to do work at his headquarters, but to go over the whole district, to see for himself the state of the people, and to make sure that all the officers under him are doing their duties properly. Again, even in a small district he cannot do his work properly if the population be excessive. In Oudh there are 522 inhabitants to a square mile, in Bengal 471, while in the Punjab there are only 188, in Sindh only 60, and in Burma only 35.

Much also depends upon the character of the people in the district, upon their neighbours, and upon the laws and conditions on which land is held, for these differ very greatly in different parts of the empire. If the people are lawless and turbulent, or if their neighbours belong to some native state which is not well-governed, or if they are savage tribes, then much of the time of the ruler must be spent in restraining disorder, and much of his attention must be given to the affairs of the neighbouring state. He will devote more care and more time to his police arrangements than would be needed in an orderly, peaceful district with good neighbours. So, too, the time and attention he has to give to his revenue duties depend largely upon whether he has to collect revenue from a few large landlords or zamindars, as in Bengal, or from a large number of raiyats, as in Madras. Considering the work that has to be done, the administration of each of the 259 districts requires, on the whole, about the same amount of care and attention from the officer in charge of it. If it should be found, after a time, that the work in any one district has, from any cause, *e.g.* a rapid increase in population, increased largely and become too heavy for one officer to manage, a new district is formed by taking away parts of the larger and more populous districts.

64. **The district officers**. To administer, that is, to govern each district, and to manage its affairs, there is a staff of officers, each of whom has his special

work, and all of whom but one—the civil judge—are under the orders of the head of the district, who is called the collector. The district officers are, in addition to the collector and judge, the assistant-collector and deputy-collector, the superintendent of police, the executive engineer, the civil surgeon, the superintendent of the jail, and the forest officer. They are all district officers, but as the collector is the chief of them, he is sometimes called *the* district officer. Besides these, there are officers whose work lie in more than one district, and who move over three or four districts, which make up their circles or divisions. These are the inspectors of schools and salt or abkari revenue, and in some places the survey officers.

65. **The executive.** These district officers are the most important of the executive officers of government, who are so called because they *execute* the orders of the central government, and carry out the decisions and sentences of the judges who administer the laws of the country. Above them, there are higher officials who overlook their work, issue orders and transfer them, as there is need, from one district to another. The district officers are well known to all the villages and towns in the district which they visit on their frequent tours. Upon them, depends the success of the government. If they are active, honest, and clever the district will be well governed, for however excellent the orders may be which are issued by the central government, who make laws and rules at the capital of the province, the government of the district cannot be good unless these orders and rules are obeyed and carried into effect. To see that this

is done is the duty of the district or executive officers.

66. **The collector.** The term collector came into use a long time ago under the East India Company, when the chief duty of this officer was to collect the revenue. The word 'governor' would at the present time describe far better the rank that he holds and the duties which he has to perform. He is, however, still called collector in Bengal, Bombay, Madras and Agra, while in the Punjab, Oudh, the Central Provinces, Burma and the smaller provinces he is known as the deputy commissioner. People cannot feel any strong attachment to a mere term such as 'government,' but a living governor, in their midst, they can regard with feelings of personal affection or respect. The collector has, and it is right that he should have, very great power and authority, for he is to the people in his district their Ruler whom they can see, and hear, and obey. The affection that has often been felt and expressed by simple Indian villagers for a just, wise, and kind collector is well known. In the large district of Khandesh in the Bombay presidency the collector, Mr. Propert, was always called by the people Raja Propert, and before his time Sir James Outram had even to a greater degree won the affections of its inhabitants.

67. **Majesty of the law.** No laws, rules, or regulations are made by the collector and his subordinates. That work is done by the governor of the province and his council. Their duty is to execute these rules, to see that they are carried out and obeyed. Neither have the collector and his assistants the power of

judging in civil cases. That work is done by the civil judges and the officers under them. When the British began to rule the country and took charge of the districts from the native rulers who were there before them, they found that there had never been any distinction made between the duties of a judge and those of an executive officer. There were no written codes of law, such as we now have, in British India, laying down the way in which taxes are to be collected, or providing for courts of law, or the working of municipalities. In the old days the native kings and chiefs were despotic rulers. They issued their commands, and those commands were the law.

In Asiatic countries it has always been thought that the king is not bound by any law. In his own kingdom he is above all law. He kills whom he wills, and whom he wills he keeps alive. Everything in his kingdom belongs to him, even the lives and the property of his subjects. No doubt there have been a great many good rulers in India, and if the rulers were good, and just, and kind, like Asoka or Akbar, then the orders which they issued would be good, and the people would be happy and contented, and the country prosperous. But, on the other hand, a good ruler was often succeeded by a bad, or lazy, or weak ruler, and then the people were badly off. And even under great and good kings the district officers ruled without much control, one reason being the difficulty, in former times, of communication. They did pretty well what they liked. They executed their chief's commands, and at the same time they were the judges in all disputes among the people. There could be no appeal from them except to the chief himself. If the chief oppressed his subjects, they could not call him before any court of law or complain of his treatment to anyone.

CHARLES I. OF ENGLAND, EXECUTED 1649.

Even now, in many of the native states of India there are no laws except those made by the chief, and there are no judges distinct from the executive officers. These officers cannot be called before any court of law to defend their action as officers of the government. In some of the larger and better governed states, such as Mysore and Baroda, the British system is followed, for this was introduced when British officers had charge of the government for a time and in many others there is a gradual change taking place in imitation of the plan followed in British India. The British government were the first to introduce into India the rule that all officers of government, even the Governor-General himself, the Governors, and all subordinate to them must obey the law, and to entrust the making of the laws, and as far as possible the interpretation or the application of them, to persons who are not themselves charged with the duties of enforcing the laws. There are not many countries in the world where the law is held in such honour and esteem as it is in Britain, where even the king must obey its commands. More than once in British history a king who broke the laws of the country was dethroned; and one king of Britain was tried, found guilty, and executed for breaking the laws while Shah Jehan was reigning in India.

68. **Duties and powers of the collector.** As soon as the districts taken by the British had settled down to peace and order, and civil government was firmly established, a collector and a judge were appointed, the collector being the chief executive officer and the judge the chief judicial officer. All officers but the judge are under the orders of the collector, who is the head of the district. He has in the first place to collect the revenue and the taxes according to the laws, and so far as this part of his duties is concerned he has what is called revenue jurisdiction, sometimes deciding what taxes are due and at other times hearing appeals against the decisions of his assistants. He is also the district magistrate hearing appeals from the magistrates subordinate to him, and arranging for the disposal of their criminal business. Should

he, however, act illegally by imposing a tax contrary to law, or by passing an unjust sentence in a criminal case, his actions can be referred to a higher authority. He controls the work of the police, and if necessary he calls in the aid of soldiers to keep the peace in his district. He has to care for the comfort and well-being of the people, to help the engineers with his advice as to what roads, canals, bridges, and public buildings, such as schools and hospitals and offices, are wanted; he has to assist the civil surgeon with his opinion as to the steps that should be taken to prevent sickness, and to advise the inspector of schools in many matters connected with education. He has to report to the Governor of the province as to when self-government should be given to those towns which are without it. Often he has to look over buildings in which manufactures of various kinds are carried on, to see that the workpeople are properly treated and the machinery in proper order. If the rains should fail and there should be any signs of famine, it is the duty of the collector to keep the officers at the head of the government fully informed of the state of his district.

The proper working of every part of the government of the district depends upon him. If anything goes wrong, it is his duty to put it right if he can, and if not, to report it at the headquarters of the government to some one above him who is able to do so. He has to spend a good deal of time in touring over the country in order that he may know as much as possible about it. He is in this way able to see how the officers under him do their work, and to listen, in person, to any complaints or suggestions which the people may wish to make. Whether the work of all the other officials in the district is done properly or not depends very much upon the energy and personal character of the collector, for they are very likely to follow his example.

69. **The collector's assistants.** It need scarcely be said that it would be very difficult, if not quite impossible, for the collector to do all his work himself, without any help. He has assistant collectors and deputy collectors to assist him. If the district be very large, it has one or more subdivisions each of which is in charge of one of these assistants, who is called the subdivisional officer, and does the same kind of work as the collector, under his orders. One of them is, as a rule, in charge of the Treasury at the headquarters of the district. In those provinces which have deputy commissioners, the assistants are called assistant commissioners.

70. **Other district officers.** The civil surgeon has under him the large hospital at the chief town in the district and the smaller hospitals or dispensaries in other places, which altogether number 2500 institutions giving treatment to 23 million cases in British India in a year. The civil surgeons are chosen by competitive examination, and some of them, as well as the majority of the medical officers in charge of dispensaries, are natives of India educated in the medical colleges. The British government pays great attention to the health of the people, but this was thought to be a matter of no concern by the former rulers of India. It is, however, beginning to receive

attention in the native states. The executive engineer has under him a large number of assistants who have been trained to their work in government colleges. In every part of the country the roads are now many more in number and very much better than at any former time in the history of the country. All the

WALTER HOSPITAL.

large rivers are spanned by magnificent iron bridges. The roads in British India are equal to those in any country of Europe and far superior to those in any other country in Asia. Nothing has done more for the prosperity of the country and the comfort of its inhabitants than the network of roads that overspreads the country.

71. **Divisions and commissioners**. In all the larger provinces, except Madras, three, four, five, or more

districts form a group called a division, which is in charge of a commissioner. There are, altogether, 53 divisions in British India. The commissioner is placed over the collectors, and has to overlook the work of the district officers in his division. He has no executive work himself. All letters and reports from the district officers to the central-government officers at headquarters pass through his hands, and he gives his opinion on every important matter. In some provinces there is also a Board of revenue which relieves the government of much work, and in Madras the Board, consisting of four selected collectors, also takes the place of the commissioners, all letters on revenue matters to the local government passing from the districts through their hands.

72. **Taluks or parts of the district**. The provinces are, as we have seen, divided into districts, of which there are 259 in British India. In the same way, each district is, except in Bengal and Burma, sub-divided into smaller parts which are called tahsils, taluks, or tálukas. These divisions into tahsils were originally made chiefly with the object of collecting the revenue. In Bengal, where there is a 'permanent settlement' of the revenue, the districts are divided for police purposes into thanas, under thanadars. In Burma, the tract under a myo-ok or township corresponds to the tahsil, but it is again subdivided into revenue circles under a thugyi, each circle including several villages. There are five or six, and sometimes more, taluks in a district. Each of them is in charge of a native officer called a tahsildar, and in some parts of the country a mamlatdar and in Sindh a

mukhtiarkar. He is to his taluk what the collector is to the whole district, the ruler and chief executive officer, and his duties are as many and as various as those of his chief. The tahsildars are chosen with great care, and are most important and able servants of goverment. The proper working of the rules of goverment in the taluk, the protection of the villagers from hardships and oppression, and their general well-being depend very greatly upon the zeal, the honesty, and the ability of the tahsildars. They are now almost entirely natives of India, and generally they have obtained degrees at some university. Until such men were available these posts were largely filled by Europeans, often promoted from the offices of the collector; but as the supply of native graduates increased, the administration of the parts of British districts rapidly passed into their hands. Those who aspire to be collectors must enter the civil service by passing the competitive examinations open to all British subjects throughout the world, and held in the capital of the British empire at London.

CHAPTER VII.

THE SUPREME GOVERNMENT.

73. **Government—central and local.** We have seen that all the towns and villages in British India are grouped into 259 districts and that each district is complete in itself, being ruled by its collector

and his officers, who act as they think right and according to law, or else execute or carry out the orders of the central government, and are therefore called the executive. The districts again are grouped into provinces. At the head of each province there is a Governor in Council or a Lieutenant-governor or a Chief Commissioner. The Governor, assisted in the presidencies by two members of council, and in the other provinces exercising sole authority under the title of a Lieutenant-governor or a Chief Commissioner, but in all cases working through secretaries at the head of each department of the government, is known as the local government or administration. Just as the collector administers the district and gives effect to the orders of the local government, so the local government administers the province and gives effect to the orders of the supreme government. The provincial governors are aided by legislative councils in the larger provinces when laws have to be made, but otherwise upon them alone rests the whole responsibility of governing their provinces. In some matters they have only to execute the orders of higher authority, namely, the government of India, in all other respects they themselves issue orders and make rules for every matter which concerns their provinces or any portion of them. If, then, we gain a clear idea of the part taken by the supreme government, we can understand the duties of the local governments. For, whatever the supreme government does not order or arrange, that the local government has to do.

The system of divided authority is extended still

further within the province. It has already been shown that in large towns municipal boards or councils manage the government of their towns in such matters as concern those towns alone. And in each district, and in many of the taluks or tahsils, there are also local boards to which are entrusted the management of such matters as affect their own district or taluk alone. Even the villages—each village for itself, or a group of small villages—have sometimes their own panchayats and govern themselves in matters which concern themselves alone.

Thus the village in some matters rules itself and in others is ruled by the tahsildar or mamlatdar of the taluk, who executes the orders of the collector. The taluk, through its local board, in some matters governs itself and in others it is governed by the collector of the district through the tahsildar. And in the same manner the district in some things rules itself through its local board, and in others it is ruled by the collector who executes the orders of the provincial government. Thus in the village, the taluk, and the district, there are two kinds of authority side by side, the one being exercised on the spot and applied to local affairs, and the other introduced from above and carried out by officers, acting as agents of a distant and higher governing power.

74. **Why there should be supreme control.** Our first step towards understanding the plan of government is to see what part the supreme authority in India must itself take in the affairs of the provinces. In each province there are matters which are local,

that is to say, matters which concern it alone and have nothing directly concerning other provinces. The province of the Punjab, for example, has nothing to do with the roads, the tanks, the schools, the canals, the hospitals, or the methods of field cultivation in Madras. But there are other matters which

TYPES OF THE BRITISH ARMY.

equally concern both provinces. Letters are sent in large numbers from the Punjab to Madras and from Madras to the Punjab, and from one town to another and one village to another, all over India, at a very low charge. A letter or a post-card may be sent for three pies for a thousand miles. It goes quite safely and very fast over this enormous distance; and, in this way, millions of letters are sent.

In order to prevent mistakes, and to correct a

mistake, as soon as possible, very great care is wanted, and all the arrangements must be made by one central office which gives its orders to the smaller post-offices all over India. If the ruler of the Punjab made his arrangements to suit his own province alone, they might not work well with those made in Madras.

TYPES OF INDIAN CAVALRY.

Lord Dalhousie therefore decided that all postal arrangements both in the Punjab and in Madras, as well as in every part of India, should be under the direction and control, not of the ruler of any one province, but of the ruler of the whole of India. The same thing is true of the telegraph department and of the great state railways. It was chiefly the fact that there was no strong supreme ruler over all India that made travelling and the sending of letters or money from one part of India to another so difficult in former days. Rich men travelled in the disguise of poor men, or took with them a strong guard, for they were afraid of being robbed or made to pay heavy tolls or give large bribes as they went from one petty kingdom to another, or even from one large city to another. This we know from many accounts written by early travellers in India.

Again, the army, which protects India and keeps the peace all over the continent and watches every point at which a foreign foe might break through to invade the country; and the fleet of war-ships which keeps the coasts safe both from the attacks of enemies and from sea-robbers, must also be under the orders of the supreme ruler of India. In every province troops are stationed, they are paid for by taxes levied in every part of the country, and they would be sent to defend any part which might be attacked. The sea-port cities on every part of the coast are kept safe by our navy from invasion by sea, and savage and cruel enemies who might break over the border and overflow the whole country are kept at bay and forced back by the soldiers and line of forts in the north-west of India. An enemy who might invade the Punjab would be met, not by soldiers under the ruler of the Punjab only, but by soldiers who would be rapidly sent up from every part of India. This could only be done by one supreme ruler of India.

It is also necessary that treaties should be made by the supreme government. A long time ago, before the Regulating Act was passed in 1773, each presidency was independent. There was no Governor-General of India before Lord Clive in 1765. The consequence was that the ruler of one presidency made a treaty with the ruler of a native state who was an open enemy of the ruler of another presidency, and much mischief followed. If the fourteen provinces were now to be, in the same way, independent of one another, and under no supreme control, the same thing might happen again. Moreover, now that the whole of British India is subject to one King-Emperor, Edward VII., there ought to be some one to act in his name when treaties of any kind are to be made with another country or a native state. Only the ruler of the whole country can do this. A treaty made by a provincial governor might be disputed by neighbouring states.

The ruler of each province very properly does all that he can for it. Sometimes it may happen that what may be very good for one province may not be quite so good for another, or may even harm it. A province situated on the coast, with good harbours, visited by numbers of trading ships, might, if it were left to do what it liked, try to enrich itself by taxing goods which had to pass through it in order to reach other provinces inland. Or one province may frequently suffer from famine because of a failure of the rains, and its revenue may consequently be small, while another may always have good crops and its revenue be very high. It may be necessary to help the poor province by giving it some of the revenue of the rich province, and this can best be done by a central government, which has no preference for one province over another and can act for the good of the empire as a whole.

Again, although each province has its own rules and regulations in all matters that concern itself alone, yet it is right and proper that in all provinces in British India the same general rules, the same laws, and the same general policy and system of work should be followed.

For all these reasons it is necessary that, in all matters which concern the whole empire, and may therefore be called imperial instead of provincial, there should be no confusion or risk of contrary orders being given by different rulers, and each local or provincial government should be under the orders of one supreme ruler. At the same time, in order that this ruler of the empire may be able to give his whole time and attention to those matters alone and not be distracted by having to attend to other things, it is equally necessary that he should allow each provincial governor to rule his own province, with the aid of his councillors or his subordinates, and give orders and make rules in all those matters which have to do solely with the province.

75. **Supreme rule difficult in former times.** The great Moghal emperor Akbar and his successors attempted to rule their empire in the same way, but they had not the advantages we now have of good roads and railways and telegraphs. Orders could not then be sent to any part of India as they now can in an hour or two. The subadars or governors of provinces were left too much to themselves. They obeyed the emperor only when they chose to do so,

and he often had to send an army against a rebellious governor to force him to obey. When Aurangzeb died and the next emperors proved weak and incapable, several powerful subadars threw off the control of the emperor and founded kingdoms of their own in Oudh, Hyderabad, Bengal, and elsewhere. These subadars had been given too much power, and had been left too long in charge of their provinces. No English governor or general in the British service has ever been known to try or wish to found a kingdom of his own in India. The British governor comes out to India, stays for a fixed period, and then returns to his own country.

LORD MINTO

76. **The Viceroy.** The supreme authority in India itself is the government of India, a body consisting of 8 persons, at the head of which is the Governor-General, who, since the transfer of India to the Crown, has also been called the Viceroy; and he represents His Majesty King Edward VII., the Emperor of India, in all public ceremonies and acts. If a treaty has to be made with a foreign state binding the King-Emperor it is signed

by the Viceroy, or if a foreign prince, or a member of the royal family visits India, the Viceroy receives him in the place of the king. Again, in times of great danger the Governor-General may pass an ordinance or law without the aid of his council for making laws, and in certain cases, fixed by the law of Parliament, he may act alone in opposition to his Executive Council. But these powers are exceptional, and the Governor-General is not intended to use them unless grave necessity arises; and even then his powers depend upon the law and are exercised in accordance with the law. As a general rule, the government is carried on by the Governor-General and his members of council acting together. The Governor-General usually remains in office for five years, being appointed by the Crown, that is, the king of Britain. Although he is a statesman of high rank and reputation, he could not alone do all the work connected with the government of India. This would be beyond the power of any one man, however strong and able he might be. To help him he has two councils, one called the Executive Council, which conducts and manages the affairs of government, and another called the Legislative Council, which makes laws for the whole of India. The Viceroy and his Executive Council make up the body of men known as the Government of India, or the Supreme or Imperial Government.

77. **The Executive Council of the Viceroy.** There are six ordinary members of council, who, like the Viceroy himself, usually hold office for five years and are appointed by the Crown. The commander-in-chief

of the army of India is usually an 'extraordinary' member. If the Governor-General should require to be absent from his council on tour an Act may be passed conferring upon him alone some of the powers of the government of India and leaving others to his councillors. On the other hand, if the Governor-General in council should meet for business in Bombay or Madras, the governor of that presidency would attend the council as a member. This occurred when Lord Northbrook proceeded to Bombay to prepare for the visit of the present King-Emperor, who was then Prince of Wales. Two of the ordinary members are usually senior officers of the Indian Civil Service. One is a military officer of high rank. One is an experienced lawyer, who is usually sent out from England, and another is specially charged with the advancement of trade and commerce. The sixth member must be skilled in finance or accounts. He may be an Indian civilian, or he may be sent out from England.

78. **The Viceroy's Legislative Council.** The work of this Council is to make laws and regulations for the whole of India. It includes the Executive Council and some other members, called the additional members. In 1902 the Legislative Council contained twelve additional members, of whom three were official and nine non-official. Before any law is made, it is fully discussed in the Council. Any non-official member may give his opinion on it. The financial statement for the coming year, which gives a full account of the income which is expected from taxes and other sources, and the expenditure, or the various

ways in which it is intended to spend the income, is also placed before the Legislative Council, and any member may ask any question he pleases regarding this statement, and give his opinion upon it or upon any part of it.

79. **The Secretariat.** All the work which has to be done by the government of India is divided under seven heads, corresponding with the Viceroy and his six or seven councillors, which are called 'departments' or parts of government. Although the orders finally issued are the orders of the whole government, yet it is convenient for each member of council to have charge of one of the departments of state, and in that branch he transacts his business, with the secretary to government, who in turn is helped by a number of assistants and a large office. All the secretaries together make up what is called the Secretariat. These departments are (1) the home, (2) revenue and agriculture, (3) legislative, (4) finance, (5) military, (6) foreign, (7) public works and trade and commerce. The division of the military work of the government of India into two departments, of which one would be under the commander-in-chief as extraordinary member of Council, is a subject now engaging consideration. The Viceroy himself takes the foreign; another member the home, revenue and agriculture; the legal member, the legislative; the financial member, finance; and the commander-in-chief and the military members deal with the military departments.

80. **Headquarters of the Viceroy.** The Viceroy and his Council have their headquarters at Calcutta or

Fort-William from November to April, but between April and October they reside at Simla in the Punjab. A provincial government could not do its work out of its own province, nor a district government out of its own district; but the Viceroy, who rules not only one province, but all India, is at liberty to reside in any part of India which he finds to be most suitable and convenient for himself and his Council. The Viceroy and the members of his executive council occasionally make short tours and visit different parts of the country to see for themselves how work is being done.

81. **Government in public.** One point in which the present government of India differs from every other government that has gone before it is that it makes known to the people all that it does. All the laws, the acts, the rules, the proceedings of government, whether of the supreme, the provincial, or any local government or local board, are published in the different government gazettes. All laws and important rules that government proposes or intends to make are published in draft form long before they are actually made, and every newspaper in the country gives its opinion upon them, so that government knows what the people think of them. If there is any way in which they can be improved or any want supplied, this can be done before the law is passed. Even the resolutions of district boards and those of the humblest taluk boards are published, both in English and the vernacular. All the accounts of the empire, full details of every way in which the money of the people is spent, are published for their information. Every-one who can read knows exactly what is being done.

All is open and above-board. Nothing of this kind was ever known in former days. It would have been regarded as a crime to find fault with government or even to pass an opinion on its actions. One of our chief authorities for the events of Aurangzeb's reign was a writer who assumes the name of Khafi khan, "Sir Secret," and his book was not published till the mighty emperor had passed away. Abul Fazl, it is true, in his work the *Ain-Akbari*, gives us an account of the empire in the days of the great and good Akbar, but it is what we should now call a gazetteer, written once for all, and very different from the regular annual, monthly, and even in some cases weekly, reports and gazettes of our present government, which give the people at large every detail of what has been done.

82. **Imperial duties.** The government of India is the supreme power in India, standing in the place of the King. As in the old times and under native rule any one who was oppressed might complain to the king, so at the present day any person or body of persons, who think that they have been treated unfairly or unjustly by any of the provincial or local governments, may 'appeal' or complain to the supreme government. Such appeals must be made by means of petitions. There are rules which show how these petitions should be written, and in what way they should be sent up to government. Considering petitions of this kind and passing orders upon them is a large part of the work of the supreme government. As this work has to do with 'appeals, it may be called 'appellate' work.

But besides dealing with appeals which relate to work which has already been done in the various provinces, there is a great deal of business which has to be done entirely, and from the beginning, by the supreme government, and which, as it is first or originally done by them, and not merely referred to them by other governments, may be called 'original work.' As we saw before, it is business which concerns all provinces equally, that is to say the whole of India; part of it relating to the Native States and part of it to British India. It may be divided under the following heads:

i. Foreign affairs, including the declaring of war, the making of treaties and arrangements, and the appointment and supervision of political agents or consuls in foreign parts or native states;
ii. The military, naval, and marine forces;
iii. General legislation, or the making of laws;
iv. General taxation;
v. Currency, or the making of money, and the public debt;
vi. The post-office, telegraph and railroads;
vii. Emigration;
viii. Mines and minerals.

83. **Foreign affairs.** Some parts of India touch countries that are ruled by great European powers. On the north-west there is Russia, on the north-east there is France. Their territories in Central Asia and in Siam come right up to India. The empires of Persia and China, and Afghanistan are also close neighbours. When two countries touch one another there

is always a good deal of communication and trade between the natives, and to prevent quarrels between them it is necessary to have fixed rules which both nations will agree to keep. These rules are put into agreements and treaties which are made between the rulers of the two countries. If they should be broken there is always the risk of war. To make these agreements between India and its neighbours, to see that they are kept and to write letters about them in such a way as not to offend the rulers of the countries to which they are sent, requires very great care, knowledge, and experience. It is clear that important business of this sort can only be entrusted to the highest authority, for foreign rulers expect to correspond with none but those who have power to bind their countries. Therefore the supreme government, with the Viceroy at its head, undertakes the direction of foreign matters, and even in India itself deals with the most important of the native states, appointing and controlling the political officers. Again, in the case of the native states under the local governments, great questions, especially those involving new engagements or interference, must be settled by the Governor General and his council.

84. **Military and marine forces.** It is equally necessary that the government which makes treaties should be strong enough to make other powers keep them, and to have under its orders an army and fleet with which to make war, if war should be necessary. Again, we must remember that any enemy of India is also an enemy of Britain. Both countries are very closely connected and are under one King. The whole

power of Britain is behind India, and would be put forth, if necessary, to defend India. If the government of India declares war, war is really declared by the King of Britain, and in such matters as war and peace the Governor-General can alone take action under the authority of the British government at home. Many years ago, before the telegraph lines connected India with London, the Indian government sent a mission to Persia and then prevented a mission sent out from England from going there, acting in each case without the permission of the authorities at home. So too in India the government of Bombay entered into agreements with the native states of which the Governor-General disapproved. To prevent such mistakes the supreme government keeps in its own hands complete control over the armed forces, and the Viceroy is responsible

ONE OF THE VICEROY'S BODYGUARD.

to the Secretary of State in London for his actions. In the last century there were three armies in India, and in the presidencies of Madras and Bombay there were local commanders-in-chief. Such a division of authority only weakened the armed strength of government, and it is now recognised that an army or a naval force should not only be directed by one central authority, but that the same authority should in times of peace organise and prepare it for war.

85. **Other work of the supreme government.** The Council of the Governor-General makes all laws which apply to the whole of India and those regarding the general taxes and accounts of the whole country. It also makes all laws for the smaller provinces which have no law-making councils of their own. Since no part of government can be carried on without money, the supreme government raises what money is wanted by fixing the rates at which taxes are to be paid, and making such laws as may be necessary to enable each province to levy these taxes. It also fixes the share which each province may keep, for its own expenditure, out of the taxes it levies, and the share which must be given to the supreme government for the maintenance of the army and the performance of the various duties which devolve upon the government of India. It prepares the 'budget' or statement of accounts, including the estimate of money which it expects to get, and the expenditure already made on various objects. It carefully notes the state of the accounts from month to month so as to lessen

expenditure if need be, and thus make sure that only so much money is spent as is actually available. It also has under its care the making of coins in the mints and the issuing of paper-money or currency notes. And if any provincial government wishes to borrow money, it must first get leave to do so from the supreme government.

Departments like the post and telegraph and railway, which carry on their work in every part of India, are also under its direct management, for this work can be done by it better and more cheaply than by any local government. Lastly, the supreme government does work for each province in all cases where it is necessary to collect information throughout the empire, for local governments could not easily get this information from district officers who are not under their orders. Therefore the supreme government obtains the accounts of the trade which is carried on everywhere, showing what things are exported and imported, and their value; and it collects from places inside and outside of India information about the wind, the tide, and the rainfall. It also fixes the terms upon which persons may look for metals and minerals anywhere, and the tax which those who own mines must pay to government for working them.' In short, the government of India is conducted in the same way as a large bank or firm of merchants is worked. Its business is done partly at headquarters and partly at branches in various parts of the country. All general rules are made by the head office, which keeps the accounts of the whole business, while each branch is left at liberty to make its own rules for its own special local work.

86. **Provincial governments.** We have seen that the supreme government of India does a part of the work of government itself, and divides the work to be done between various classes or departments of the Secretariat. The local governments follow the same rule, although it may be necessary with them for one secretary to take charge of two or more departments. These departments are, as it were, channels which carry the same class of business from all the villages or towns of India, through the district, and the province, and so on, if necessary, to the same department at the headquarters of the central government. The provincial or local governments perform their duties in the same way as the Governor-General in Council, and once it is understood that certain matters must be settled by the central authority it follows that all other matters must be decided and arranged by the local government. The latter in its turn transfers to its agents part of its authority, and even the municipal and local boards possess no powers which are not derived from the government. One and all from the central government to the village headman are responsible to the law and the King for the discharge of those duties which are entrusted to them.

87. **The Secretary of State for India in Council.** In 1858 the Parliament of the United Kingdom transferred the government of India from the Company to the Crown, and replaced the court of directors, and the board of control which used to

supervise their proceedings, by a Secretary of State for India aided by a council. All the revenues of India and the property of the directors were transferred to the Crown or the Queen of the United Kingdom in trust for the welfare of India, and these revenues cannot be spent without the sanction of

HOUSES OF PARLIAMENT, LONDON.

the Secretary of State and a majority of his council, which consists usually of twelve members, most of them selected for their experience of Indian administration. The Secretary of State is responsible to Parliament for what he does. He is a member of the 'Cabinet,' which includes the Prime Minister and those members of Parliament who directly conduct the government of Great Britain. The Secretary of State in Council conducts all business which is done in Great Britain in connection with India. He presents to Parliament every year a 'Financial Statement' showing the income and expenditure in India under various heads, and also a 'Statement of the moral and material progress and condition of India.' His sanction is required to declare war, and he must inform Parliament when he gives this sanction, and, except to actually repel an enemy or prevent the invasion of any part of India, no money can be spent, out of Indian revenues, on any war outside of India, without the consent of Parliament. Every law passed by the Legislative Council of India must be reported to the Secretary of State, who has power to leave it alone, or advise the King-Emperor to disallow it. He may give orders to any officer in India, including the Governor-General, and he may dismiss any officer from the service of government. He also advises the King-Emperor on the appointment of a Governor-General, a Governor of Madras or Bombay, a judge of a High Court, members of council, and certain other high officers of government. But just as the local governments govern the provinces, notwithstanding the powers of the supreme government, so the Governor-General in Council governs India whether he acts on his own authority, or executes orders received from London. In India itself he is the supreme ruler, or, as his name indicates, governor in chief, held in check by the law and by the Parliament of the British nation, which, by its votes, may upset cabinets and secretaries of state. India thus shares indirectly all the benefits of the free British constitution. The chain of authority may be a long one, but its links are unbroken and stretch from Westminster to every Indian village.

CHAPTER VIII.

LEGISLATION.

88. **The making of laws.** It has already been shown that one of the chief differences between the two systems of government, in native states and in British India, lies in the fact, that laws in the former are made in private by the executive government, and in the latter by bodies which, being in one respect independent of the executive authority, discuss their business in public. This freedom and the publicity of the law-making authority are important matters, and so contrary to the spirit and customs of Eastern countries that they were only gradually introduced into British India. In 1600, Queen Elizabeth of England gave a charter to the East India Company by which it might make laws for its own servants. Sixty years later, King Charles II. authorised the Governor and Council 'to judge all persons belonging to the said Governor and Company, or that should live under them, in all causes, whether civil or criminal, according to the laws of the kingdom.'

Thus English law was introduced into India within certain narrow limits. In 1765 the Company became the rulers of Bengal, and in 1772 Warren Hastings made a code of laws called Regulations for Bengal. The next year, in 1773, the British Parliament passed the Regulating Act, which founded a Supreme Court in Calcutta, and gave power to the Governor-General and his Council to make regulations for the good order of Fort St. William and places subordinate thereto. In 1793 it was decided that all laws should be printed and published, that they should be translated into the vernacular languages, and that the grounds or reasons for each law should be clearly stated and prefixed to it, and that all laws should be formed into a code. This revised code was commenced in 1793 for the regulations of the supreme government, and in 1802 and 1827 for Madras and Bombay respectively.

In 1833, on the renewal of the Company's charter, the Governor-General was empowered by Parliament to make laws for the whole of India, for all persons, British or native, within the Company's territories, and for all servants within the native states, thus depriving the presidencies of Madras and Bombay of their legislative powers, but leaving their governors the right of proposing laws for their own provinces. A fourth member was added to the supreme council, to assist the executive members in preparing and making laws, but he was only permitted to sit and vote when the council met to pass laws; he took no part in the executive business of the government. The laws passed since 1833 are known as Acts.

Each Act is now referred to by its number and the year in which it was passed. In the same year, 1833, a law commission, of which Lord Macaulay was the leading member, was appointed to make recommendations, and after some delay its labours led to the enactment of the great penal code of India. But before that happened Lord Dalhousie had, in 1854, introduced great changes into the legislative business of India. He enlarged the legislative council of India, bringing to it members from the presidencies and judges from the high court at Calcutta. Its discussions were printed in neat volumes, similar to those which recorded the proceedings of Parliament, and its deliberations were conducted with great ceremony, so as to increase the dignity and independence of its members. After the mutiny, an Act of Parliament was passed, in 1861, which gave back to the presidencies the power of making local laws taken from them in 1833, and introduced additional members, both official and non-official, into the councils. The whole course of proceedings was then carefully laid down so as to secure the fullest discussion and enable the opinions of the public to be taken upon schemes of legislation. Legislative councils have under the law and its amendments been given not only to Bombay and Madras, but also to Bengal in 1862, to the United Provinces in 1886, to Punjab and Burma in 1897, and to Eastern Bengal and Assam in 1905.

89. **The Council's Acts.** The Act passed in 1861 was amended at various times in 1871, 1874, and 1892, so that, as education and intelligence spread in

India, larger powers might be given to British subjects in the matter of helping the Government to make and improve the laws. Thus in 1861 the Governor-General was allowed to add to his executive members of Council, not less than six, or more than twelve additional members, 'for the better exercise of the power of making laws vested in the Governor-General in Council.' These members were to be nominated by the Governor-General, half of them being non-officials, that is, persons who are not in the civil or military service of the Crown in India. In 1892 the number of additional members of the Council of India was raised to a minimum of ten and a maximum of sixteen, those of the presidency Councils being made not less than eight or more than twenty, and the maximum for the United Provinces being fixed at fifteen. The same limit is laid down for the new province of Eastern Bengal and Assam, the number of official members being not more than seven. But a more important change was made in the selection of some of these additional members. The nomination still rests with the Governor-General, or, in the case of the local councils, with the Governors; but the public are invited to select suitable persons for nomination, with the object, as the Secretary of State wrote, 'of bringing the legislatures into closer relation with the best representatives of public opinion in India, and of multiplying the opportunities for an interchange of views and information between the governments and their councils.'

Under the rules formed with this object five of the seats on the Council of the Governor-General are made on the recommendations of the non-official additional members of the councils of Madras, Bombay, Bengal and the United Provinces of Agra and Oudh respectively, and of the Calcutta Chamber of Commerce. In the various provinces other systems of election are followed, so as to give municipalities and local boards, or large societies of landowners, or merchants, representation; and to secure full opportunity for discussion, great importance is attached to publicity and ensuring a correct report of the proceedings. For this purpose Bills or proposed Acts are carefully drafted by a special official and then published. When all governments or public bodies interested in the Bill have been consulted, and its clauses have been translated into the vernaculars, it is considered by a committee of the Council, who report upon it. If it is altered by them it is again translated and published in the official Gazettes, after which process it is discussed and amended in the Council; and finally, after open debate, it is passed or rejected. Then it receives the sanction of the Governor-General, or, if a local Act, also that of the Governor. Finally it is reported to the Secretary of State for India, as will be explained presently. In the main the system is the same for local legislatures, although the number of additional members and the mode of choosing them varies.

But there are limits to the laws which the local legislatures may pass, and also to those which the Council of the Governor-General may pass. The latter may not pass laws which affect the authority of Parliament or the British or Indian constitution, and the former cannot, without express sanction, even consider laws affecting the public debt or the imperial taxes, currency, post office, the penal code, the discipline of the armed forces, the relations of government with foreign states, or the religion of any classes of His Majesty's subjects in India. The main principle is that the provincial legislatures should deal with provincial matters, although in some cases where a new principle is sought to be applied to one province only, even that law is discussed in the Council of India.

90. **Right of interpellation.** Two other changes have been introduced into the law of 1861 which deserve notice. One concerns the discussion of the financial statement, and the other deals with questions put to the government regarding public affairs. We shall learn more in a later chapter about the income and expenditure of the government. Every year the authorities calculate what they expect to receive from taxes, and how they mean to spend what they get. As the year advances, they correct their estimates by the state of the public purse or treasury, and when the year is over they still further correct their revised estimate by the light of facts, and in a statement show the actual budget or receipts and expenditure of the past year, and the probable income and expenditure of the current year. This statement is explained every year in the Council of India, and any member may then offer any remarks upon it that he pleases to make. If he criticises any part of it, the member of the Executive Council in charge of the finances makes his reply; and thus the public, who read the discussion, have an opportunity of learning all about the revenue, and how it is spent.

In the provincial Councils a similar opportunity is given to their members. But the law goes further than this. It allows members of the various Councils to ask questions of which previous notice is given. Such questions must be framed so as really to elicit information, and would not be answered if the president of the Council thought that public interests would be injured by giving the information asked for. For instance, it would be dangerous to discuss foreign affairs, or to give to the public information that might lead to war, or weaken the defence of the empire. The questions and the answers given are recorded in the proceedings of the legislatures, and thus become known to everyone.

91. **Special ordinances.** We have seen how the laws of India, called Acts, are passed by assemblies after open discussion, and with intervals of time between the debates intended to secure full deliberation. But if grave disorders should occur, there might be no time for such debates, and it might even be dangerous to allow discussion. Every government is bound, in case of grave danger or emergency, to take extreme steps to maintain peace and order. Accordingly, in such exceptional cases the Governor-General may publish ordinances which have the effect of law for six months unless the King-Emperor refuses to allow them. It is only necessary to add that all acts, regulations, or ordinances, however passed, must be reported to the Secretary of State for India, who, if he thinks fit, can advise the King Emperor either to leave them in force or to refuse his assent to them.

CHAPTER IX.

RACES AND POPULATION OF INDIA.

92. **What makes a country strong and prosperous?** The strength and prosperity of a country depend partly upon its position, partly upon the qualities of the people who inhabit it, and partly upon its natural capabilities and resources, such as great rivers, fertile soil, rich mines, large lakes and extensive forests. A country can never be rich if it be a rainless desert, and even if it be fertile and have lakes, rivers, forests and mines, it never can be wealthy and prosperous so long as it is inhabited solely by savage tribes often at war among themselves or fighting with their neighbours. The most prosperous nations are those which are most highly civilised, where full use is made of the natural wealth of the country by its inhabitants.

So vast is the extent of India, stretching as it does over thirty degrees of latitude, and so varied is its surface, including lofty mountains, deep rivers, high hills and wide plains, elevated table-lands and fertile valleys, that we find in it more variety of climate and soil than in any country in Europe. And, with these varieties of climate, there is a rich abundance of the products of the earth, including nearly all those of mild, temperate countries as well as those of hot tropical climates. India ought, therefore, to be one of the richest countries in the world, for it has very great natural advantages.

In past times the people of the country were not able, from various causes, to make the most of them. One reason was that the citizens of India used to be shut out from the rest of the civilised world, and therefore unable to benefit by the inventions of modern times. Another was that wars constantly raged in many parts of the country. Countless numbers of the people were killed, and homes and villages laid waste, so that the natives of the country were not able to make much progress in studying the character and extent of their possessions, and turning to account the natural powers of the soil, or the riches buried below its surface which were waiting to be used by man. Only when there is perfect peace at home and absolute safety from attack from abroad can arts and manufactures, commerce and trade, flourish. It is not until quite recent times that proper advantage has been taken of the resources of India, either of its mineral wealth—coal, iron and gold—or of its vegetable products, many of which grow in few other countries—indigo, tea, coffee, cotton, opium, tobacco, and rice. The present is the most favourable period that has ever been known in the history of India for the development of its resources.

93. **Famine less to be feared now than formerly.** It is true that the rains do not always fall at the proper season; and, when this is the case, crops cannot be grown, and there is famine. Such is the vast extent of India, however, that if there be famine in one part plenty of food is produced in other parts. In former times India was divided into a great many

kingdoms, and when famine prevailed in one of them no help was given to it by others, and the people died by millions. But the whole country is now under one rule, and all parts of it are equally cared for, so that scarcity or famine in any one of its 259 districts is met from the full crops of other districts, and food and money poured into it.

And India, being a land of lofty mountains, is also a land of mighty rivers. In the north, the valley of the Ganges, which is fed not so much by rain as by the melting of the Himalayan snows which never fail, and in the south, the valley of the Caveri, are among the most fertile valleys in the world. Vast quantities of grain are grown in these well-watered regions. And besides the old rivers there are now over 40,000 miles of canals which run like new rivers over wide tracts of country and water millions of acres. Even now vast quantities of water rush down to the sea and are lost. If all this water could be kept back and made to run over the face of the earth, millions of additional fields could be watered.

The canals which have been already made are every year being added to, and in time we may hope to see a network of them all over the country. But there must always be some limit to the extension of works of irrigation, because they cost a great deal to make and to keep in proper order, and the cost of them may be so great that the money received from the sale of the water may not suffice even to pay a small interest upon the outlay. Some works in fact do not even pay for the expense of their annual upkeep. In addition to canals many tanks have been excavated or repaired, and thousands of new wells are dug every year by the help of government. Quite lately successful attempts have been made, by boring deep into the earth, to bring to the surface, through narrow pipes, stores of water that lie far below. These artesian wells may be made in many places where no water comes into ordinary wells.

94. **Position of India.** A country lying next to powerful states, with no strong barrier between them, is always in a dangerous position, for it may easily be attacked. Great Britain is much more safely situated than most countries, for it is an island, and to attack it the invader must cross the sea. France and Germany touch each other, and often has France invaded Germany and Germany France. Only 35 years ago the armies of Germany overran France and took its chief city Paris. If we look on India as one great continent we shall see that it is to a large extent protected by nature from attack by a foreign enemy. On three sides there is the ocean. The British navy, which is by far the strongest in the world, would prevent any hostile force from being landed on the eastern, the western, or the southern coast. From the rest of Asia, India is cut off by the great mountain ranges of the Himalayas, which, like mighty walls, stretch across the north for more than a thousand miles.

It is true that on the north-west and on the north-east there are passes through which, in bye-gone days, invading armies have again and again poured down into the plains of northern India. On the north-west Aryans, Greeks, Tartars, Scythians, Afghans, Persians and Moghals have at different times burst into India through these passes and overflowed all northern Hindustan; while through the openings in the hills on the north-east, by the Brahmaputra valley, the Mongoloid tribes of Central Asia have again and again come down into the rich countries around the delta of the Ganges, where their descendants now live. It would be a task of much difficulty to invade India now, so long as the military forces are properly maintained. The passes are carefully guarded by strong forts and a powerful army. British soldiers, with their native comrades, Sikhs, Rajputs, Pathans, Punjabis and Gurkhas, would be ready at once to resist any invaders, who might seek to cross the land frontiers of the empire for purposes of attack.

95. **Diversities of race.** We learn from history that different races of mankind have special qualities. Some are by nature good soldiers, others make good sailors, some excel in agriculture, and others in trade and commerce, some are good miners, others good artizans. The most prosperous nations are those in which all these and many more classes of men are found. Such nations contain, in themselves, all the classes and castes of men that are needed to supply the wants of the whole community. They do not need to send to other countries for them.

If we search the whole world through we shall find no braver or better soldiers and sailors, no more active traders and manufacturers, no more wealthy or enterprizing merchants, no more skilful farmers, no cleverer engineers, doctors, and men of science generally than are to be found, at the present day, in India. They are drawn largely from the native races of the country, and they include as well many of the ablest representatives of the strength, the skill and the science of Great Britain.

96. **The population.** The population of India is vast and varied. It is made up of many different races of men who have come into the country at various times and made it their home. There were by the census of 1901, in round numbers, 294 millions, of which total 232 millions inhabited British India and 62 millions the native states. Classified by religion, they included:

Hindus, - - - -	207 millions.
Muhammadans, - -	62½ millions.
Buddhists, - - -	9½ millions.
Christians, - - -	3 millions.
Sikhs, - - - -	2 millions.
Jains, - - - -	1⅓ millions.
Parsis, - - - -	94 thousand.
Animistic (aboriginal tribes),	8½ millions.

The *Aborigines* are the descendants of the first inhabitants of India. At first they probably lived in the plains, on the banks of the rivers. But as other and stronger races came down into the country, they fled to the hills, where they are now found. There are nearly 9 millions of them, and they speak many different languages. The chief of these tribes are the Bhils, the Kandhs and the Kolis. As they differ so much from one another in colour, features and appearance, as well as in languages and customs, it is clear that they must be of different races; but where they came from, and when, and to which of the great families of mankind they belong, it is hard now to tell. They are wild and poor, and have very little to do with the other people of India. They are strong

A NAGA CHIEF.

and hardy, and have very good sight and hearing. As time goes on, and they become civilised, they will, no doubt, take their places in the great Hindu community and work for the common good of the country.

The *Hindus* number about two-thirds of the total population. They, too, include numerous races and castes, which differ in colour and features, in the shape of their skulls, and in height and appearance, and speak many different languages. At the top of these numerous races are the Brahmans and higher castes, which claim descent from the Aryans, who six thousand years ago slowly drove their flocks and herds through the rocky gorges cut out by the Indus and its tributaries into the Punjab. They brought with them civilisation and introduced a settled government into India. After dwelling for a long time in the Punjab, they gradually spread over the whole country and subdued the numerous tribes whom they found there, mixed with them so as to form one people, and introduced their own language and civilisation. As the ages rolled on, other races—Greeks, Scythians, and probably many others of whom we have no record—followed, settled down among the Hindus, adopted their language, customs and religions, and took their places among the natives of the country. To the Aryans and their Hindu followers the continent of India owes its first lessons in civilisation and agriculture. They changed the wild races of hunters, who were the only inhabitants in former times, into a society of orderly citizens, and made the country rich, populous and civilised.

The *Muhammadans.* But the richer a country is, the more tempting it becomes to invaders. When the Aryans had, in the course of ages, spread over Hindustan, cut down the ancient forests, brought large tracts of country under cultivation, built large cities, and introduced order and civilisation everywhere, they lost the strength and vigour which had made them able to subdue the aborigines. The Brahmans had ceased altogether to handle the sword and the spear, and had become a caste of scholars, priests and law-givers. The great masses of the population, the mixed castes of the Sudras, had wholly given themselves to the arts of peace, to agriculture and trade. The Rajas and their fighting men, the Kshatriyas, and in after times the Rajputs, were still, no doubt, well able to keep the peace in their own countries, and were the bravest warriors of their time within the limits of Hindustan. But they were as unable to contend with the big white men who lived in the countries to the north-west of Hindustan and passed their lives in fighting, as the dark-skinned inhabitants of ancient India had been to contend with their own fair-complexioned Aryan fore-fathers thousands of years before. Fresh sets of in-vaders from Central Asia, Persia and Afghanistan—Arabs, Turks and Moghals—all fierce Muhammadans, filled with zeal for their faith, and eager for plunder and spoil, swarmed down one after another into Hindustan and gradually took into their hands the government of nearly the whole country. They supplied fresh fighting blood to the nations in the north of India, and so active were they in spreading their faith that at this day there are about 63 millions of Muhammadans in India, more than a fifth of the whole population.

After living, however, for generations in the hot plains of Hindustan, the once hardy Muhammadans, the Pathans and Moghals, shared the fate of the Hindus. They, too, lost their old strength and skill

A RAJPUT WARRIOR.

in arms. When Nadir Shah, the Persian, invaded the Moghal empire in 1739, it was found that Hindus and Muhammadans were alike powerless to contend with him. Twenty years later, when the Marathas had become the strongest native power in Hindustan, Ahmed Shah, the Afghan, led an army of hardy soldiers down into North India. The great Maratha chiefs assembled in their hosts to drive him back, but their efforts were in vain. Their might was shattered on the field of Panipat, their leaders killed and few left alive to tell the tale.

The *Parsis* number only 94,000 but they make up one of the most important communities in the country. Over a thousand years ago when the Arabs conquered Persia, and compelled the inhabitants of the country to become Muhammadans, some of the Persians fled from their native country and took refuge on the western coast of India. The Parsis are their descendants. Hindus have for ages been unwilling to cross the ocean to trade largely with foreign countries, and, although the Muhammadans in the West of India carry on trade with Africa and Arabia, yet, as a general rule, both Muhammadans and Hindus confine themselves to the internal trade. But the most important part of a country's commerce is that with other foreign nations, and in this the Parsis have always taken the lead. They are one of the wealthiest and best educated of the peoples of India, and, small as their numbers are, one of their community sits in the British Parliament as the representative of a London division or constituency. These native merchants of India benefit artisans and manufacturers by selling their goods for them. They are also manufacturers themselves. Some of the largest cotton mills in Bombay belong to them. And they are as generous as they are rich. A benevolent Parsi gentleman quite lately gave 30 lakhs of rupees to found an art college for the benefit of his fellow-citizens.

Europeans. There are only about 170,000 Europeans in India, men, women, and children, of whom 70,000 belong to the army which defends India.

97. **Dangers which beset India.** We learn from history very clearly that there were three great dangers to which the lives and property of the people of India were exposed before British rule began. These were that the coasts of India were open to attack by sea, that the country was exposed to invasion by the passes in the North-West, and that the fighting classes, whose duty it was to defend the country, had become unable to do so by long residence in it. It may be added that all classes lost many advantages, which civilised nations in modern times enjoy, by being cut off more or less from the rest of the civilised world.

Each one of these dangers and disadvantages has been removed by the coming of the English into the country. The sea-coast is protected by the English navy. The North-West frontier is guarded by English and native troops, well-armed and disciplined, and supported by all the aid which modern science can give. The British soldiers come from their native cold country in the North of Europe, and do not stay long in India. After three or four years of service in India they are sent back to Britain, and their places taken by fresh soldiers. All the numerous comforts and conveniences of modern Europe are now brought to India in British ships, for everything that has been discovered or invented in modern times is to be found in Britain, from whence it comes to India. The number of British inhabitants in India is but small, and few of them, even in civil employments, spend all their lives in the country. They often go to and fro from Britain to India, and when they finally leave, their places are taken by fresh Britons who have all the strength and vigour of their race, and bring out with them the latest knowledge from the colleges and schools and workshops of their country.

In the days in which we live, the fate of a battle is decided far less by personal strength and valour than by skill, discipline and the use of the best weapons. No doubt if both parties in a war had equally good weapons, the braver and stronger would win in the end. But the strongest and bravest men, if ill-armed, would have no chance against trained soldiers armed with the best modern rifles and artillery. Certain races and castes in India have always been known as martial or fighting castes. They are as a rule those who live in the cooler portions of the continent especially in the hilly tracts. Such are the Sikhs, the Rajputs, the Gurkhas and the Marathas among Hindus, and the Punjabi Muhammadans and Pathans. In South India there are the Coorgs and Mappilas. To render them efficient against a foreign foe, however, they need to be well disciplined, well armed and well officered. It may be added that they should be well housed and well paid, so that they need not be anxious that their families will come to want while

GURKHA SOLDIERS.

they are away on military duty. When they grow too old to fight, they should be given pensions so that their last days may be passed in comfort. In most of these points no provision was made for the armies of former days in India. The Marathas were not soldiers by profession. A part of the year they spent at home cultivating their fields. At the end of the heavy monsoon rains, they set out on an expedition at the call of their leaders, and returned to their homes when it was over. The Rajputs did the same. And the soldiers of Akbar and Aurangzeb were not paid and pensioned as the soldiers of the Indian Army are at the present day. Even such pay as they were promised was often months or years in arrears. If soldiers are to fight properly they must be constantly trained in the art of war, well led by intelligent officers, and punctually paid their proper wages.

The native soldiers who now defend India are all trained men, soldiers by profession. Their lives are spent in constant preparation for war. They fight when it is necessary to do so, shoulder to shoulder, with their English comrades, who come from over the seas where the climate is cool and bracing. They are led by well-trained English officers. They are well housed and clothed and cared for in every way, and are armed with the best weapons that can be made in Europe. They are employed by a government which they can trust and which pays them regularly. For 150 years no foreign enemy has invaded India, and there can be no doubt that any enemy, who should venture to come, would be resisted by soldiers determined to preserve their liberties and privileges as citizens of India.

CHAPTER X.

TRADES AND OCCUPATIONS OF INDIA.

98. **Division of Labour.** The masses of the people in all countries support themselves and their families by work of some kind, and out of the money which they earn they give a part, called a tax, to Government, in return for which it affords them equal justice in the law courts, maintains order throughout the country, and ensures their protection by soldiers and police. Nothing, therefore, is of greater consequence to the people and to the Government than a steady supply of work. Such work should be of as many kinds as possible, and everybody ought to be free to choose that form of work which he likes best, or that by which he can, from time to time, earn most money. If, for instance, Indian workmen did nothing but till the soil, their hands would be idle whenever it pleased God to withhold the rains, or if the crops should be destroyed by locusts, or floods, or in any other way. It is, therefore, very important that Indian workmen should have other ways of earning a living than by ploughing and sowing.

Again, if one kind of work can no longer be done, or no longer gives any profit, then the men who used to do it ought to be able and willing to turn their hands to other kinds of work. To take one instance, the trade of the Banjaras, or carriers of goods on pack saddles, came to an end when roads were made and carts introduced. There was a still greater change when canals and railways were made. People who want to fetch goods from a distance or to send them to market will not pay heavy charges for a slow and costly way of carrying them when they can save both money and time by using carts or canals or railways. These means of moving from place to place and of conveying goods from one part of the country to another are of great use to all classes of people, and, therefore, it is only right and proper that they should have them, even though one class, the Banjaras, suffered by the change. But even the carriers themselves were not long in finding some new way of earning a livelihood. In every prosperous community there will always be improvements in the manner of doing work or carrying on trade, so that workmen and merchants must alter their methods or change their trades. It is, therefore, most desirable that there should be ready for all as many different kinds of work as possible.

And it has been found that it is not wise for Government to make laws or rules which prevent men from engaging in any work which they prefer, or in any trade which suits them, or from doing such work in any way they like. No doubt Government ought to see that those who employ workmen take proper care to protect their lives and bodies from serious injury or disease. It is one of the duties of Government to take care of the lives of the people and protect them from harm. This is why people pay taxes. But having done this, government need not

BANJARAS.

interfere any further between workmen and their employers, or attempt to fix the rate of wages paid for any kind of work, or the price which may be put upon goods of any kind by those who sell them. If one trade decays and another thrives, the people themselves are the first to find out and to feel the change, and as each man knows for himself, far better than government, the sort of work which best suits him, he should be left free to do whatever work he likes.

99. **Capital.** There is, however, something which a government can do in order to help people to find labour. In any large trade or manufacture two things are equally needed—namely, capital and labour, in other words, money and men. Government can, by maintaining peace and justice, encourage those who have money—capitalists—to begin a manufacture and employ artisans and labourers. For countless ages there has been a considerable quantity of gold lying deep in the earth in the Kolar district of Mysore State in South India. In old times the people of Mysore collected gold from the surface of the fields or dug it up from a few feet below. They carried the gold which they picked up straight to the goldsmiths or traders, who paid them on the spot for their labour. But a time came when the native miners could dig no deeper, and for hundreds of years the work stopped. There the gold lay, deep in the earth, and there it would still be lying if British capitalists had not provided the money for bringing out from Europe skilled engineers to teach the native miners how to work, and machines for getting up the gold ore and for taking the gold out of it. Hundreds of thousands of native workmen have been given work which is well paid, and they, their wives and their children, numbering many hundreds of thousands more, have

been fed by this new industry, while millions of rupees' worth of gold, lying idle and unable to be turned into money for commercial purposes, have been won from the earth for the use and benefit of man.

This one instance shows how capital which came from England has benefited the people of India. The capitalist runs some risk of losing his money altogether when he starts a new industry of this kind, or of not making any profit on his capital. In fact he frequently fails owing to difficulties which were not foreseen when he began to spend his capital on the enterprise, and if he fails, the loss falls upon him alone. But whether he fails or succeeds, he benefits the people whom he employs by paying them for their work. And he sets an example which is of the greatest use to Indian capitalists, for although they may be afraid to risk their money in a new and untried industry, they can and they will gladly follow where others show them the way, and imitate a successful enterprise.

There are many other home-industries in cotton, tea, coffee, cinchona, jute, indigo, iron, coal, paper and silk which have in this way been opened to Indian workmen by the aid of capital from Britain. Nearly all the railways in the country have been built in the same way. A country may have large natural resources, there may be untold wealth lying in the soil or below the surface, but without capital its inhabitants cannot make use of them, and they are as badly off as a country which has none. For this reason the Bombay Presidency Association, in preparing an address to the Queen-Empress Victoria on the completion of sixty years of her reign, pointed out that one of the greatest benefits that India has received has been the flow of British capital into the country. They wrote as follows:

"In all these various ways the peace and prosperity of the country have been promoted, with the result that during the past sixty years the population has multiplied nearly 100 per cent., cultivation has extended so as to keep pace with this growth, and trade and commerce have flourished beyond all previous measure, and been beneficial both to England and India. India has become the chief customer of British manufacture and trade, and it affords a safe investment for the employment of nearly 500 millions of British capital in the development of Indian agriculture, manufacture and trade. The bonds which unite the two countries have thus become indissoluble, and under British protection the various races of India, speaking different languages and professing different creeds, have learnt to feel for the first time that the connection between the two countries is a providential arrangement intended to weld them altogether into a great Indian nation, owning common allegiance to the same sovereign, and having common interests in the promotion of peace and goodwill throughout the land."

100. **Occupations.** According to the last census, out of 294 millions nearly 192 millions were supported by agriculture, and if we add to the cultivation of the soil some twenty-five occupations which are closely connected with it, nine persons out of ten in India are so supported. More than 11 millions of people,

including their families, were engaged in spinning, weaving and cloth making, and nearly 4 millions in working up metals and stones. On the other hand, the persons, including all the members of their families, who were supported by the public service or employed

INDIAN PLOUGHMAN (MADRAS).

in the service of self-government boards and of native states numbered only 5 millions. Thus it appears that agriculture supports the vast majority of the people of India. In reality it supported a far larger number than 192 millions, because those employed in the care of cattle, to the number of 4 millions, the preparation of food-stuffs (16½ millions), and the construction of carts, also live on the cultivation of the soil, although they do not actually plough and sow.

The great difference between India and Great Britain lies in this, that the mass of the people of India depend upon the crops of the country, and therefore on the seasons, while the British not only import their food, but also the raw material of their industries, and work it up for the market. India sends cotton, indigo and timber to other countries, where skilled artizans manufacture them into various articles for the use of mankind. Since the monsoon rains may fail in many parts of India, and crops may be attacked by locusts or ruined by floods, the British government has always done all that it can to open out to its labouring population new ways of earning a livelihood and of obtaining wealth. This is done so that too many of them may not depend upon the cultivation of the soil, and that some of the working classes may be able to support themselves by work, which will not stop even if the rains do not fall at the proper time. The requirements of government are very small as compared with those of private persons, but, so far as it can, government helps Indian manufacturers by buying from them, whenever they can produce goods as cheap as those made in Britain or other countries. Much of the paper now used in government public offices is made in Indian mills, and Indian coal is chiefly used on state railways.

101. **Mines.** We may mention a few of the ways in which new employments have been created. Beneath the soil of India lie many of those metals and minerals which have made England and other countries rich and industrious. But before the establishment of British rule there was no one in

India willing to risk his own money on the undertaking, nor able to induce others to do so, neither were there skilled engineers who could do the work. Although the coal-fields of India, as far as they have been explored, cover an area of 35,000 square miles and contain 20,000 million tons of coal, yet until quite lately, all the coal wanted for the railways, steamers and factories in India was imported from England or Australia or Japan. But India now gets from the Bengal and Singareni and other coal mines 7½ millions of tons annually, and about 100,000 workmen are employed in this work, which does not depend upon the rainfall. To these 100,000 must be added the families they support, and there are, besides, a great many others who earn a living by carrying coal to other places, and by trading in it.

Coal will in future be a source of great wealth to India, for there is enough not only to supply all that the country wants at present, but all that it is ever likely to want, and, in addition, the wants of other countries. Coal can be sold at a large profit in other countries of Asia. In 1902, over 500,000 tons of coal, worth 38 lakhs of rupees, were exported from India. Ten years before this, in 1892, 640,000 tons of coal were imported into India, but in 1902 only 230,000 tons were imported. Indian railways now use Indian coal almost everywhere, only 1 per cent. being imported coal. Coal has been found in every part of India except Bombay, Mysore, and Sindh.

India has also plenty of iron, whole hills and

ranges being full of ore of the purest varieties, and with cheap coal it may be able to produce steel and iron for its railways, its factories, and its buildings. The gold mines of Mysore have shown what capital and European skill can do for the country. They are now giving annually 650,000 ounces of pure gold taken from mines which Indian workmen, left to themselves, were obliged to abandon. The Mysore government does not spend a rupee upon the works, but is paid by the companies of capitalists 17 lakhs of rupees a year for leave to work the mines. This is called a royalty, and is much the same as a tax. Besides, the Mysore government gets a large revenue in other ways from these mines, while an army of native workmen, paid by the British companies, are supported in comfort with their families.

102. **Tea and coffee**. Without capital and labour no country can get rich, for without men to work and money to pay them, it could not be made to produce anything. But something else is also wanted. Just as necessary as these are skill and experience to find out what new products can be grown, what articles can be made in it, and to introduce industries from other countries. When the first English settlers arrived in Bombay, they found it a sandy waste. Within a few years they had brought the Persian rose and other shrubs and flowers from neighbouring countries, and had adorned the settlement with the beautiful plants and flowers for which it has since been famed amongst the cities of the East. Their example has been followed by their successors. In 1820, some European planters settled in Mysore

and in the Wynaad, and they set to work to convert these hilly jungle-tracts into coffee gardens. About the year 1830, in the time of Lord William Bentinck, government began the attempt to introduce into India the cultivation of tea. Men were brought from China to show Indians how to grow the plant and prepare the leaf. For many years the results proved poor, but patience and perseverance were at last rewarded. Having shown others how to do the work, government then left it to private capitalists. This is how the great tea industries of India and Ceylon began. They now supply nearly the whole of the tea drunk in Great Britain. Just as the people of India buy one third of the total of the cloth goods exported from Lancashire in the year, so the British consumer buys from India four out of every five pounds of tea which are annually exported from it. Every Englishman, young or old, consumes on an average six pounds of tea in the course of the year, and his wants in this respect, which used formerly to be supplied by China, are now met by several hundreds of thousands of Indians engaged in the plantations of Assam and other provinces of India. Thus we see how each nation assists the other by its industries. The Lancashire operative, living in a cold, inclement country, clothes the people of India by his industry, while ,the native of India, able to work in the field, provides the British workman with corn, tea, rice and other products suitable to the soil and climate of India. There are other articles, such as tobacco and sugar, which would be more freely bought by Englishmen if the Indians were more careful in their methods of preparing them for the market. It should be noticed with regard to tea and coffee that employment is given not only to the local residents of the districts in which they are grown, but also to a large number of labourers imported from Bengal and other

COTTON GOING TO THE MILL.

parts of the country where the population is excessive and work difficult to find.

103. **Cotton.** But the most striking of all the benefits which British capital and British experience have conferred upon the workmen of India is the establishment of the cotton industry. For many years the only cotton mills in the British empire were those in England. Englishmen then opened cotton mills in India. The example they set was soon followed, and

for some time past both Parsi and Hindu capitalists have worked mills of their own in Bombay and other cities. At the beginning of the nineteenth century there were few things made in India which were valued in other countries, except Dacca muslins, dyes, and pottery. But India has now, of late years, taken rank as a manufacturing country. It can boast of about 200 cotton mills worked by steam, which employ 179,000 hands, so rapidly has this single industry grown since the first mill was introduced by the British in 1854. These mills supply the country largely with cotton clothing and also export piece goods to Japan, China, and other Asiatic countries.

104. **Other industries.** India supplies the world with jute. From it are made the 'gunny' bags in which corn and other grains are carried from country to country. In 1903-4, the value of jute exported from India was 2 crores of rupees. Formerly raw jute was sent to England and there made up into bags, but now the jute mills of Bengal are as important as the cotton mills of Bombay. They make up into bags nearly half the jute grown in the country. Large quantities of jute bags are needed in India itself for carrying grain. These are all now made in Bengal instead of being imported as formerly. Jute is cultivated in more than 2½ millions of acres, and about 118 thousand persons are employed in the 36 jute mills of Bengal.

Besides cotton and jute mills there are many other mills classed under some 50 different heads, among them being bone crushing mills, cement works, chemical works, lac factories, oil mills, potteries, tile factories, sugar works, tanneries, rice and flour mills, paper factories, saw mills, and indigo factories.

The silk industry is being taken up, and in many other ways skilful and experienced British capitalists, who do not mind risk, are trying to introduce fresh manufactures and trades into India, so as to give work to natives of the country. The 'trade returns,' or accounts published by government, which give details of the trade and commerce of the country, and the figures in the census reports, where the occupations of the different classes of the population are given, show plainly what great changes are being made in the lives of workmen. They are earning money in many different ways which their forefathers never even heard of. It is not only the working classes who benefit. The wealthy classes, instead of burying their money in the ground, or buying jewels which yield no return, now invest their money in manufactures or trades which give them large profits. It was owing to the importance of trade and industry to India that Lord Curzon created a new department in charge of a member of council whose time should be given to the improvement of this branch of the administration. The chief centres of Indian industries are the seaports, the provincial capitals, and the railway centres. In Howrah, a suburb of Calcutta, 10 per cent. of the people depend on jute mills and presses, while in Bombay and Ahmedabad cotton mills, and in Rangoon rice mills, support respectively 15 and 11 per cent. of the population.

105. **Government service.** In talking of the

occupations and careers open to the people of India we must not forget appointments in the government service. But these are much fewer in number and less in value than those offered by the great professions and industries, which not only employ far larger numbers of men, but also pay them salaries and profits much larger than public salaries. Government appointments do not increase in number and value as fast as those connected with business and commerce. It is true that as population increases and trade extends, more courts and more public offices are needed. But, on the other hand, the government of the State is giving more and more power to municipal and local boards, and these boards appoint their own servants.

It often happens that some of the highest appointments which government can bestow, as, for instance, a Judgeship of the High Court, are declined by successful barristers, to whom they are offered, because they find that they can make a much larger income by practice at the bar than they would get from the salary of a judge. A successful private doctor will make more than the pay of a district surgeon. Much more money can be made in the larger banks, in mills, and by buying and selling shares on the Stock Exchange, than the income from pay in the service of the State. In the old times in India, as at the present day in Persia, China and other countries close to India, public servants were allowed to trade and receive large presents besides their pay. They also had very large powers over their fellow-countrymen, which added to their dignity and importance. At the present time, however, under the British government, all public servants are strictly forbidden either to trade or take presents of any kind. They get a fixed salary, and they must obey the law like everyone else. They have no more power than private persons, except what the law gives them.

Nevertheless, the service of government is honourable, and it carries a pension with it, and although many able men prefer business or a profession to it, there is keen competition for every government appointment. When we see how eager young men are to enter the government service, we ought to bear in mind that the State, after all, can employ a very small part of the population of India. In the whole of India the total number of government civil appointments, with a monthly salary exceeding 75 rupees, is 28,280, more than half of which are filled by Hindus, 42 per cent. by Europeans and Eurasians, and 7 per cent. by Muhammadans. Of Europeans alone about 6,500 are employed in the administration as against 21,800 of the inhabitants of India itself. But even if we take the full number of officials receiving the salary stated, we must at once feel how few they are, and how a single industry like cotton can do more to find work and profit for the population of India than government can do with the whole of its public appointments.

106. **Emigration and factory laws.** We have seen that if the industries of the country are to prosper people must be left free to do whatever work they like to do, and that if people are to be always profitably employed, they ought to be able to turn their hands to some new work if their old work ceases to

be profitable. The less the State interferes the better. Whatever one class of workmen may lose by the decay of any trade will be made up to it by the opening of another and more profitable business. If things can be made by machinery in some new factory cheaper and better than they can be made by hand, it is a clear gain to the mass of the people who require to buy those things, while the few workmen who formerly made them by hand can find some other way of earning a living, often in the very factory where the manufacture has been taken up. So long as peace is maintained in India and capital is provided to pay for labour, whether it be sent from other countries, or provided by wealthy Indians willing to spend their own money on new industries, fresh occupations are constantly being created.

Government must, for its part, attend only to the main objects of keeping the public peace, improving the means of communication and giving all the information required by capitalists who may wish to introduce any new trade or manufacture. But when government has done this it may wisely leave labour to itself. To this general rule there is one exception. When foreign countries wish to employ Indian labour, as in the case of Demarara, Trinidad, Jamaica, Mauritius, Natal, Fiji and Surinam, the British government takes care of emigrants and enforces rules for their comfort during the voyage and for their safe return with their earnings. In the same way it protects labourers who go to Assam or elsewhere if it be necessary. The only object of government is to prevent any ill-treatment of the labourers or any misunderstanding between them and their employers as to the agreement they make. Sometimes the government does a little more than this, as in the case of factory laws, so as to protect the weak and young from being given harder work than they can do, or to guard against accidents which might be caused by badly-made machines.

107. **The value of freedom.** The chief reason why the British government has been so successful in multiplying the occupations and industries of the empire is that it has given freedom to labour—freedom to labourers to do what they like, on whatever pay they can succeed in getting,—and freedom to employers to employ whom they like, on whatever pay they think they can afford to give. No man can compel another to work for him and no man can compel anyone to employ him. A good and kind master will always find servants to work for him, and good, active, honest and skilful servants will always find masters very glad to take them. From the year 1843, when slavery was abolished in India, government has never changed its rule of maintaining peace and the freedom of labour, and trying to attract British capital so as to give the population other means of livelihood besides those which the cultivation of the soil may afford.

CHAPTER XI.

THE PUBLIC PEACE.

108. **How the peace is kept at home and abroad.** The first duty of those who rule a country is to preserve peace and order within the country itself, and to guard its frontiers by land and sea so that no enemy from without may be able to enter and invade it. For the former purpose, governments employ a civil force, called the police, and for the latter they rely upon their army and navy. It is of the highest importance to the people that both these forces should be perfect in every way, so that they may be quite able to do the work for which they are intended. The greatest blessing that a country can have is peace, and the greatest curse under which it can suffer is war. We, who have known only peace all our lives, can scarcely imagine how dreadful a thing war is.

What would happen if there were to be civil war in our country, or if bands of robbers could roam over it at their will? In the first place, the post, the telegraph and the railway would cease to work. We should not be able to write to one another or to our friends in distant places as we do now, nor should we be able to travel about from place to place. Almost every kind of business would come to a standstill. Goods could no longer be taken from town to town and from village to village, nor could supplies come in from other countries. Schools and hospitals would be closed. Rich men would hide their money and their jewels in holes in the ground, as they used to do in the old days, and banks would cease to work, for men would be afraid to put money into them, and there would be no money to lend out. A great many labourers would be thrown out of work, for wealthy merchants and manufacturers in other countries would no longer send capital to pay for labour in a land filled with disorder. All large factories would be closed, and even the simplest occupations would be stopped. The villagers would no longer be able to cultivate their fields, and, the crops failing, famine and disease would rage unchecked everywhere. Any one who travels across the frontiers of India may even now see a sight which was common in the heart of India itself before British peace was established, namely, frontier tribes ploughing their fields with their arms by their sides, and their ponies ready saddled in order to provide for their masters a means of escape.

Three of the forces which maintain peace and order in a country have already been mentioned. But besides the navy, the army, and the police, there is a fourth force which can preserve order in a country, and without which the best police in the world could not put down crime effectually, and that is the help of the people themselves, the loyalty of good citizens.

109. **Past and present.** What the state of India was in the dim and distant past we can only gather from imperfect records, for of early Hindu times we have scarcely any history. The very Vedas themselves, however, tell us how the Aryan chiefs fought with one another, and with the inhabitants of the country.

Those great epic poems, the Mahabharata and the Ramayana, are but histories of wars. They are filled with accounts of the slaughter of human beings in countless numbers. No doubt powerful kings may from time to time have maintained peace within their own kingdoms, but all the records we have, and the old tales of the country, show us that the continent of India has for ages been inhabited by different nations, speaking different languages, who used to look upon one another as foes. Kingdoms rose and fell, and only for a short time maintained their power by force of arms. They were constantly fighting with one another. They did not combine to help one another against a foreign foe. When the country was invaded by the Afghans and Moghals, one nation after another was overcome, because they were not united. It was, indeed, scarcely possible that they should be, for immense distances separated the north of India from the south, and the east from the west. Railroads and the telegraph did not exist in those days, and a country could be invaded and overcome long before another even heard of it.

NELSON.

From the time of the Muhammadan invasion we have a good many trustworthy histories, and they are records mainly of wars between Muhammadan kings and Hindus, and among Muhammadan kings themselves. After the great Akbar had, partly by force and partly by kindness and good rule, established his mighty empire, there was a time when over Northern India there was peace, and the people lived in safety. But from the time of Aurangzib, for the next hundred years, there were wars, bloodshed, disorder and distress in nearly every part of this great continent.

All this is changed. And the whole of India is now under one strong government. The strongest races that inhabit it are united in one great army to defend the whole country. It has what it never had before, a powerful navy. The strength of the soldiers of the nations of India is not now wasted in fighting against each other, but is reserved to repel foreign foes. If one were asked to name the chief difference between the India of to-day and the India of the past, one might say that in the past there was constant war, while now there is universal and, we all hope, lasting peace.

110. **Naval power**. Look at a map of India and you will see how large a part of it is washed by the sea. Where are the capital cities of the empire, with the buildings and factories which fill them, now situated? They are built either by the sea or a river, down which ships may sail to the ocean. If you look again at the map, you will see that from the Indian Ocean you may sail into the Atlantic or through the Red

Sea into the Mediterranean. It was in the Mediterranean Sea, in 1798, that one of the great battles was fought which decided the fate of India. It was won by Admiral Nelson, who defeated the French fleet completely, and is known as the battle of the Nile.

OFFICERS AND MEN OF THE BRITISH NAVY.

This defeat of the French prevented them from sending an army to India to help Tippu Sultan. They were unable to get to India because the British navy guarded the sea. This naval victory therefore made the work of the British army on land easier, for the French could not help Tippu. Seringapatam fell in 1799 and the ancient Hindu line of kings was restored to the rule of Mysore.

What then happened may happen again. Some

foreign foe may try to invade India from the sea, as Napoleon wished to do; so the coast must be carefully watched as well as the land frontier. The Muhammadan emperors had no navy of their own and tried to defend the coasts of India by engaging the Habshi or Abyssinian ships and sailors from the African coast. But these men became pirates and plundered the trading ships of the coasts instead of defending them. We have now an Indian marine which, with the aid of the British navy whose ships are stationed in many parts of the ocean, is able to take some part in guarding the shores of India against any attacks of hostile fleets. This has never been the case before in the history of India. Besides the navy there are hundreds of vessels belonging to several large British merchant companies such as the great Peninsular and Oriental, the British India Navigation, and others, which have a large number of magnificent steam-ships, and employ a great many Indian sailors. These ships would be useful for conveying troops and stores to India, if they were wanted, and if the British naval forces were at hand to protect them while crossing the seas. Moreover, the sailors who work on merchant ships would be of service on board the ships of war, if the necessity should arise.

111. **Naval defence of India.** There are three divisions of the great British navy which defend India. The first of these is the most distant from India and yet also the most important. It consists of the ships or fleets which are employed in the seas through which any possible enemies might have to pass.

The navy of Great Britain is by far the largest and most powerful in the world, and as large as the navies of any two European powers put together. It guards every part of the British empire all over the world, and its ships visit the most distant seas. Ships of the largest size, such as those which are employed in Europe, are never seen on the coasts of India; but some idea of their size may be gained from knowing that the largest are over 400 feet long, each of them carrying nearly 1000 officers and men and costing about one crore and a half of rupees to build. The second division of the navy includes the warships and gunboats employed by Great Britain on stations in the East Indies. Other nations—France, Italy, Turkey and Portugal—have their own ships in Eastern waters; and, in the Persian Gulf, where there is much trade and commerce from India, there are many petty chiefs who would rob and injure Indian subjects and trading ships if they were not protected by this British fleet. There were a good many pirates on this sea until they were suppressed by the British. Lastly, there is the Indian marine, under the orders of the government of India. Its ships watch the ports of India, go up and down the mouths of the tidal rivers, carry troops about and make surveys. They would also, in time of war, take part with the other divisions of the naval forces which have been described.

Few people in India understand how the country is defended by these fleets, and how the large commerce which makes it so wealthy is protected by them. In former times, before the days of fleets and navies, when ships were small and did not go far from land, the ocean which surrounds India on three sides was of itself a defence, like the moat or ditch round a fort. But at the present time, the easiest way for a foreign power to attack India would be by the sea, and one of the strongest defences which the country has is the British navy.

112. **The army.** The Indian army consists of about 225,000 men, without reckoning the Imperial service troops and the forces of the native states. Of this Imperial army, about 75,000 are Europeans, who are not kept long in the country. As fast as some regiments are sent away to other parts of the world, however, their places are taken by young soldiers fresh from England. If it should be necessary, a much larger body of men could be sent over from England to India, but the expense of the army is so great that the government wisely employs no more men than are absolutely required at the time to defend the empire. In case of need there are two other sources from which additional trained men could be obtained. They are the volunteers, who are of European extraction, and the reservists, officers and soldiers who have served in the native army. Together they number some 60,000 men. It is not on mere numbers of men, however, that we depend for our defence. However powerful an army may be, it is not of much use unless it can be rapidly moved about from place to place wherever it may be wanted. A small force that can be rapidly moved about is much more useful than a large army that cannot easily be moved. It is necessary, therefore, to have means of transporting troops with all that belongs to them, their

tents and ammunition and stores and weapons, to any part of the country.

All this we now have in India. There is a special body of officers and men called the Supply and Transport department, whose particular care it is to keep everything ready for the movement of troops. We have learnt the lesson, too, that the bravest soldiers with old-fashioned guns are powerless against an enemy armed with the latest and best rifles and cannon. The Indian army is supplied with the best weapons that are made. No doubt the forts by which India is now defended, the railways, the bridges, the factories for making guns and gunpowder, all cost a great deal, as much as it would cost to maintain a huge army. But their value as a means of defence is very great. The army which defends the whole of India, as far as mere numbers are concerned, is far smaller than the united force of sepoys which was in old times kept up by two of its chief states. But if we consider the training which our soldiers have had, the discipline which holds them together, the skill of their officers, the excellence of their weapons, and the ease and rapidity with which they can be moved, we shall see that they are vastly stronger than any army that has ever had to defend the people of India before.

113. **Armies of Native states.** From the time, over two thousand years ago, when Alexander the Great, with a small army of well-disciplined and hardy Greeks, overthrew the vast hordes of Persia and put to flight the hosts of Porus in the Punjab, it has been proved over and over again, on many a battlefield in India, that large armies without

discipline and training cannot prevail against well-armed and well-trained troops much smaller in number. By the advice of their British Residents, therefore, the Native states have ceased to employ the hosts they once did. They still have troops, but they are small in number and well-disciplined. These states are bound to defend the empire both by their treaties and for their own good and that of their subjects. Accordingly some of the leading states keep up one or more regiments for the defence of India. A British officer is lent to each of them to help them to be ready to take the field whenever they may be wanted. They are called Imperial Service troops, and number about 15,000 officers and men. They too, like the troops of the Imperial army, are supplied with modern weapons, means of transport and medical officers.

114. **Civil police.** The army has to protect us from foreign enemies, and it would also put down civil war or rebellion if this should break out. But to prevent robbery and crime and make people obey the laws is the duty of the magistrates and the police. The government might, it is true, make use of soldiers for this purpose. But it avoids that step, because troops are armed with deadly weapons which cannot be used without grave risk of killing innocent persons. Sometimes, but very seldom, if different classes or creeds, for example, the Hindus and Muhammadans in some large city, should be on the point of fighting and the police should not be strong enough to control them, troops are called out for a few hours to assist them. But this is never done unless it is absolutely necessary.

In the times of the Muhammadan emperors the

civil and military command rested in the same hands. The governors of provinces were also the commanders-in-chief, and soldiers did the work which is now done by police officers and constables. In the early days of British rule, the native system was still left in force; and even now, when a new province or district is added to the empire, order is at first maintained by soldiers. After a time, the bands of dacoits and robbers, who usually take advantage of the disorder which follows a war to roam over the country and plunder the people, are dealt with by a force which is half military and half civil. Such is the military police which is still employed in parts of Burma. Finally, a purely civil force, the police, takes their place. The civil police are usually armed only with a short thick stick called a truncheon. They are under the law like other citizens, and if they use unlawful violence, they are sent to prison. They are chosen from the ranks of the people among whom they serve. Though taught military drill and discipline, they act singly or in small parties, not as a rule in large bodies. At the same time, a few small bodies of civil police are kept available for more serious duties, being armed and drilled so that in the event of grave disorder they may act with the military forces, or else combine together and themselves supply the place of an organised military force.

115. **The policeman's finger.** In London, even at times when the streets are thronged by millions of foot-passengers and filled with hundreds of carriages moving in opposite directions and all anxious to get on as fast as they can, one unarmed constable can in a moment

stop a line of carriages or any number of people by merely raising his finger. He is able to do so because the people have a respect for law and know that the constable represents the law. No doubt troublesome persons and those who wish to break the law may at times resist him or refuse to obey him. But there are always many citizens ready to help him. Sensible people know that it is for their own good to place themselves on the side of the police, whose duty it is to maintain order. The man who refuses to obey the police, when they are doing their duty, refuses to obey the law, and, in civilised countries, most people place themselves on the side of order and help the police.

A CALCUTTA POLICEMAN.

116. **Additional police.** One great difference between the soldiers and the police is that the former are what is called an imperial force, as they defend the whole empire and are under the orders of the imperial or supreme government and are moved all over India from time to time. The latter are a provincial or

local force. They are employed by the provincial governments and, as a rule, they never leave the town or village or district in which they serve. There is no fixed proportion of police either to the population of a province or its size. The police force employed in the different provinces was in 1903 in round numbers:—in Bengal 28,500, in the United Provinces 28,000, in the Punjab 18,000, in the Central Provinces 9000, in Bombay 24,000, in Madras 24,000, and in Burma 14,000, besides the military police of 15,000. The cost of all the civil police in India, numbering with officers 147,000, including the military and village police, exceeded 4 crores of rupees.

Sometimes in a particular place some of the people who live there commit so many crimes that the ordinary police cannot keep them in order. Additional and special police are needed. But it is not fair that the inhabitants of other towns and places, which are quiet and orderly, should be taxed to provide pay for these additional police. Accordingly those who live in the place, and have either caused the disturbances or done nothing to prevent them or put them down, are properly made to pay the additional cost.

117. **The people**. There is, however, in every country one force which can keep the peace and put down all disorder better even than the army or the police. That force is the people of the country themselves. If all the inhabitants of a country were quiet, orderly, and well-behaved, there would be no need of any police at all. In almost all countries, however, there is crime, but in a civilised country, the number of good and orderly citizens is far larger than the number of those

who break the laws or live by crime. If good citizens would even help the police, as they usually do in England, when a crime has been committed and the police are trying to find out who the criminals are or to catch them when they are found, there would be less chance of the laws being broken. If they would go further and do their utmost by good advice and persuasion to prevent disorderly persons from breaking the laws of the land, they would be doing their duty as true patriots who deserve well of their country. Those who own or edit newspapers might assist in the maintenance of the public peace if they were not to allow anything to be printed in them which would be likely to stir up strife, and thus cause the laws of the land to be broken.

CHAPTER XII.

THE PUBLIC HEALTH.

118. **Science.** Every one knows that in the age in which we live great discoveries and wonderful inventions have been made, and our knowledge of almost everything has very largely increased. Things are now in common and daily use such as railways, telegraphs, and steamboats which were not even heard of a hundred years ago. Nearly all of these inventions and discoveries were made in Europe and America, many of them in England. All the knowledge and

power that have been obtained by them are at the command of our government, and are largely utilised in the defence of India. Science helps man to defend himself and to kill his foes. But, happily, science is not less powerful as a means of saving life and improving the health and happiness of mankind. It is the duty of a good government not only to maintain armies to destroy its enemies, but to do all that it can to save the lives and to preserve the health of its subjects.

119. **Ignorance.** Knowledge, however, spreads very slowly. Persons often suffer and even die through ignorance. They do not know what remedies ought to be used or where to get them. It is the duty of the government to educate the people, to spread knowledge among them, to teach them how they may check disease, and how many kinds of illness may now be cured which used to be thought incurable. If anyone should walk carelessly into an open well and so break his leg or kill himself, we should be quite right in saying that he alone was to blame for his misfortune. If a man who is very ill should refuse to take medicine which will cure him, and he dies, whose fault is it? No doubt life and death are in the power of God, but God has given to men eyes and ears and limbs and the power of reason for the very purpose of enabling them to take care of their lives and bodies.

We ought not to say that God has brought on us any misfortune if we could save ourselves from it by merely using the means of escape which God Himself has given to us. It has been found out by learned men that dirt is the cause of a great many diseases. The seeds of death lie hidden in dirty water, dirty clothes, dirty houses, and dirty streets. The Aryans of old made very strict rules as to washing and bathing, and Muhammadans believe that "cleanliness is the key of heaven." But people often forget and overlook that which cannot be seen by the naked eye. If you look at a drop of dirty water through a microscope you will see in it tiny specks which are alive. They are called microbes, and microbes like these, as learned men have found out, cause fever and cholera and plague, and other deadly diseases. A man who does not know this, and has never seen a microscope, may deny that it is true, and think that, because he cannot see with his own unaided eye these microbes, they are not there, and that drinking dirty water or washing in it cannot hurt him. He may indeed not see the specks, just as a short-sighted man cannot see a tree in the far distance; but they are there, none the less, and whether we see them or not, they kill us mercilessly. We ought therefore to be very careful not to use dirty water. The use of clean linen cloth in cleaning and binding up wounds is as important as clean water. Some few years ago certain hospitals in Europe were condemned to be pulled down and rebuilt because many patients used to die in them, and it was believed that their very walls were filled with the germs of disease, and could not be cleansed. But a learned doctor, now Lord Lister, discovered that the cause of the deaths was not in the walls of the hospitals, but in the way in which the wounds of the patients were dressed. He found out that by using very clean instruments in operations, and very clean linen cloth in dressing wounds, and by using at the same time certain 'antiseptic' or germ-killing drugs, such as carbolic acid and iodoform, the patients did not die as before but got well again, and the very hospitals which had been condemned are now among the most healthy in the land.

LORD LISTER.

These and many other discoveries which have been made by learned medical men in Europe are of as much benefit to mankind as the invention of steam-engines or the electric telegraph. Another great discovery of the nineteenth century is that of chloroform, a drug which for a time puts any animal into a sleep so sound that it has no sense of pain. Surgeons can now cut off a diseased limb, or remove an abscess in a man's liver without causing pain. Not only does the patient feel no pain, but the surgeon knows that he is giving no pain, and can therefore do his work leisurely and carefully, without the danger of a mistake being made. These new ways of saving life are now in use in India, and in each province, particularly in large cities, government has introduced them into its hospitals so as to bring them within easy reach of the people of India. We may have the benefit of them, if we want it. If those who are ill, or suffering from disease, or an accident, will not make use of the means which are before them and within their reach, it is surely their own fault if they continue to suffer.

120. **Hospitals.** When the British government began to rule in India, one of the first things it did for the good of the people was to build hospitals and dispensaries where the injured and the sick could be treated and medicines given out to them. Many of the rulers of the native States have been led to follow the example set. The people like these hospitals better and better, and every year they make more and more use of them. There are still, however, many ignorant persons in India who forget that none but the very sick go into hospital, and think that every death in a hospital is the fault of the medical officer, and is not due to the hopeless condition of the patient. Many persons go to a hospital when they are at the point of death, and when it is too late for any doctor to save them. Often they have been half-poisoned, before they go, by ignorant men who pretend to be doctors, but have no knowledge whatever of modern discoveries and methods of cure. When they find that they are getting worse they go to the hospital, but it is then too late to save their lives. If they had gone when they first fell ill, they might have been cured, like hundreds of others.

The wild tribes which live beyond the frontiers of India have great faith in European doctors. Whenever a mission is sent to explore their country or to mark out boundaries outside British India, the medical officer attached to it is surrounded at all hours by numerous patients begging him to help them, either by performing some operation, or by giving them medicine. In the same way dispensaries and hospitals on the borders of the British empire are largely attended by Pathans, Baluchis, Chinese and others, who know how good they are, and value them highly. In India itself it has been found that, the more educated people are, the more they trust in hospitals. Thus hospitals are most largely used in those provinces where education has most spread. But as any one may visit a hospital, and the friends of patients can see for themselves how the sick are treated, it is to be hoped that everywhere in India people will find out how valuable hospitals are. It is satisfactory to know that in 1902 there were over 2460 institutions under official control in British India, which received in that year nearly 373,000 indoor patients and gave relief to more than 22 millions of outdoor patients. The attendances in Madras, where there were 485 institutions, far exceeded that in Bengal, where there were 574 similar institutions.

121. **Lady Dufferin.** No one, even in Europe, goes into hospital with feelings of pleasure. People only go because they are obliged to do so, that is, because they know that if they do not they may die, and because they are sure that certain injuries and diseases can be treated there with greater skill and better nursing than they could get in their own homes. And if

men dislike entering hospitals, and only go because their reason tells them that it is for their own good to do so, much more will timid women and children be afraid of the very idea of going into them. In many Eastern countries, including India, it is the custom for women to keep indoors and never even to leave their own homes, so that it is difficult for them, even if they can overcome their fears, to go to a public place like a hospital which is open to every one who is in need of treatment. This is chiefly true of the higher classes of native ladies, not the lower and poorer classes, who do not mind leaving their own homes so much. And it is very natural for little children to be in terror at the very thought of going to a hospital, for every one knows that it is hard to make a child take medicine, even in its own home, from its own mother.

LADY DUFFERIN.

Can, then, nothing be done for women and children when they are suffering pain which medical science could remove or at least lessen? This was what the wife of the Marquis of Dufferin asked herself when her husband was Viceroy of India. 'If,' thought Lady Dufferin, 'women cannot or dare not go to the hospitals to be nursed or given medicine, cannot nurses and lady doctors from hospitals go to them and nurse them and give them medicines in their own homes?' So she devised a plan for founding in some places hospitals for women and children, where only women and children would be admitted, and for supplying there and elsewhere trained native nurses to visit those who wished for their help and advice. Both parts of her scheme have already met with a good deal of success. Nurses are being trained in several parts of India, and there is already a large demand for their services.

It is hoped that one day every large town or village in India will send to the hospitals a few native women to learn the art of nursing, so that they may be able, on return to their homes, to give help to their neighbours in time of need. In order that the plan may be successful, endeavours are made to form committees in many places to collect money by subscriptions from rich people and use it in this way. Several native chiefs and wealthy citizens are much pleased with Lady Dufferin's proposals, and have helped to carry them out in various places. There can be no doubt that when it is seen what good is being done by this nursing scheme, many others will give help too, and so place within reach of medical relief a number of sufferers whom all men ought to pity and to help.

122. **Prevention of disease**. It is better, however, to prevent diseases from beginning than to try to cure them after they have begun, and therefore the Indian governments do more than provide hospitals,

dispensaries, and nurses. We now know how certain diseases which used to kill large numbers of people in India may be prevented, or at any rate cut short and stopped from spreading.

123. **Vaccination.** Of those diseases which used to sweep away hundreds of thousands every year, smallpox was once the most dreaded. But smallpox, which formerly did as much harm in England as in India, is now seldom heard of in that country, since nearly every child is vaccinated. Just as vaccination has caused smallpox to disappear in England, so it will expel smallpox from India if all children in this country also be vaccinated. Already nearly 40 per cent. of the children born in British India are protected in this way from catching smallpox, and government is doing all that it can to put this simple remedy within the reach of every family in the land. In 1902 about seven million children under six years of age were successfully vaccinated, and the number of deaths from smallpox has very greatly decreased. Those who are good citizens will try to persuade everyone to be vaccinated who has not already been so. They may be the means of saving many a life if they will do this.

124. **Water-supply.** Many crores of rupees have been spent in the cities and large towns of India on bringing plenty of good drinking water for the people through clean channels or pipes from a distance where it can be obtained clean and pure. At first some people did not like this, because it was something new, something to which they had not been accustomed, and they did not see the good of it. But in every place, when

people ceased to drink the dirty water in the old wells and tanks into which drains often flowed, it was found that there were fewer deaths every year than before. People in other places heard of this, and began to see how necessary it is to drink clean water only. Much has still to be done to bring good drinking water into the smaller towns and villages, and all good citizens, who themselves know the advantages of good pure water, should do their best to persuade villagers to keep the wells from which they draw their drinking water separate from those used for bathing or washing purposes.

125. **Conservancy and drainage**. In the same way, both in municipal towns and villages, government is doing more and more to wash away the dirt from houses and streets through large pipes into drains. The filth in the drains is then carried away to a distance, and there burnt, or buried, or used as manure in the fields.

126. **Sanitary boards**. In order to advise public bodies or private persons how to make and keep towns and houses healthy and clean, government has in most provinces appointed a 'sanitary board' or council of health, composed of medical officers and other men who have studied the subject and know best what is to be done. In all these ways government tries to make the people healthy, and the deaths every year from cholera, dysentery and fever are now less than they once were, although they still number about six millions a year.

127. **How government fights famine**. When the rains fail and there is a famine the British government

prepares to fight against it as it would against a powerful and deadly enemy, for where an invading army might kill thousands, famine if unchecked would kill millions. So fearful a foe is famine that former governments thought that it was of no use to try and overcome it. They did not know how to deal with a vast number of starving persons, consequently they did nothing, and the people died. A great many of those who just managed to keep alive did so by selling themselves and their families as slaves to rich men, who gave them food. But the British government undertakes to help those who are in want, to feed and clothe the starving, and to send back those who are alive after the famine is over to do the same work, as free men, that they used to do before. In doing this government fights famine as it fights disease. It first tries to prevent it, but if famine breaks out in spite of all that can be done, it tries to cure the ills which it causes. To prevent famine altogether is at present beyond the power of man.

Men have not yet found out how to kill all the locusts in the country, and thus prevent swarms of them from gathering like clouds in the air and consuming the crops over vast tracts. Nor can they altogether restrain the floods of water which sometimes come down the rivers, nor even prevent a plague of rats. Still less can they bid the rains to fall, or prevent them from falling in such quantity as to flood the country. Famine must therefore come again and again in parts of India while the climate is the same. But a great deal can be done to prevent scarcity from becoming a famine, or famines from becoming so severe and causing so many deaths as was the case in the eighteenth and earlier centuries.

128. **Weather forecasts.** How, then, does government try to prevent famine? In the first place, there are officers who form what is called the 'meteorological' or weather department. They carefully watch the weather all through the year; they find out how much snow falls, how storms go through the air, how currents move in the seas and how winds blow, both in what direction and with what force. This they do in India and in the seas and countries beyond India. It has been found out by the learned that the weather has something to do with the spots on the sun, and therefore the sun-spots are also carefully watched. By doing all this, it is possible to tell beforehand what sort of monsoon is likely to fall and whether the rain will be light or heavy. If there is any danger of famine, the people are warned of it, and, if prudent, they prepare to meet the coming trouble. Government also gets ready to help the people.

129. **Irrigation canals.** Another way in which famine may be prevented is by storing up the water which comes down in large rivers, by building dams which raise the level of the stream, and thus enable it to enter channels and canals, or to fill large reservoirs and tanks from which the water is then led to distant fields as it is wanted. This process is known as irrigation. A great many canals have been made in recent years. The value of the crops grown on

irrigated lands may be judged from the fact that 15 million acres receive a supply of water from canals and yield food supplies sufficient to feed more than 80 millions of people, while in addition to these there are numerous tanks and wells all over India which can supply water for about 18

THE THREE CANALS, BEZWADA.

million acres in ordinary seasons. The Upper Ganges canal alone runs like a main river over 460 miles, and has 4480 miles of minor channels or branches. The Sirhind canal in the Punjab is 320 miles long, and has shorter channels about 2730 miles in length. The Chenab Canal, in the Punjab, has made a vast waste of sand, two million acres, into a fertile tract second to none in India. In Sindh, where the rainfall is very small, the area under cultivation has nearly doubled itself during the last 20 years.

India has now, in short, the finest irrigation system in the world. It is true that the wells and tanks may run dry in very hot seasons; but the canals may be relied upon, and they have turned deserts into gardens, adding to tracts which never before in Indian history were anything but sandy wastes some 13 million acres capable of bearing crops.

130. **Wells**. Advances of money are given by government to raiyats to enable them to dig wells. In the two years, 1901 and 1902, in the United Provinces alone, 33,000 masonry wells were dug, each of which watered on the average 9 acres. These were in addition to 284,000 wells already existing in these provinces. In Bombay, in the ten years 1891 to 1901, there were 70,000 wells dug in addition to 170,000 which were there before.

131. **Railways.** A third means of preventing famine is the opening of railways, which easily and rapidly carry grain all over India. There are now more than 27,000 miles of railway open to traffic, and some of the lines were made with the sole object of enabling food to be carried into districts which are specially liable to famine. By this means the crops grown elsewhere by irrigation can be quickly carried to the parts of India affected by drought, at times when bullocks and other animals would not be able to work owing to want of grass and also of water. The railways also enable people to leave these places for a time and go elsewhere to find work where there is plenty of food to be had.

132. **Forests.** Still another way in which government tries to prevent famine is by taking care of the forests and by planting tracts of country in which trees will grow and formerly did grow, but were carelessly cut down by the people. Where hills are covered with trees, the air just above them is cool; and clouds which the winds carry through the cool air condense, and drop rain. The air above dry barren tracts is hot, and the clouds pass without letting any rain fall. Forests also keep the soil beneath them damp, and prevent the moisture from drying up. In 1902 there were about 217,000 square miles of state forests.

133. **Freedom of trade.** In the early days of British government, when famine threatened a state or a province, it was thought that the export of grain ought to be forbidden and that the government itself ought to buy and import grain and feed the people with it. This was done, and large quantities of grain were bought by government and poured into the province, and kind persons both in England and America also sent a great deal to be given to the people. Except in places where the roads were bad or there were no railways, and where no grain would be taken if government did not send it there, it was found that this was not the best way of helping the people. Where scarcity is widespread, the help of hundreds and thousands of traders is needed. If government does not interfere, the hope of profit will induce them to buy as much grain as they can collect from outside and sell it to the people. At the same time, if all traders are left quite free they will soon compete with each other, each endeavouring to secure

some profit for himself, and so preventing any single one from charging high rates. But if government sells grain cheaply or gives vast quantities of it away, private traders become alarmed and will do nothing. Their help is lost, and public officers, being few in number and having a great many other duties to perform, are sure to find that they are quite unable to get food and give it to everybody.

No doubt government might bring a large supply of food into a particular city, but when the starving people hear that it has come they rush to it in large numbers, all order is lost, and, in their vain efforts to get what they want, numbers must be shut out and many may be trampled to death. When there is famine all over the country, relief can best be given by sending food to a great many places. This can only be done by a great many merchants, each working hard to make a profit by buying grain where he can get it cheap and selling it at a higher price, free from any fear that government will step in and undersell him or prevent him from doing as he pleases. Government, however, can and should help private merchants by obtaining and publishing for general information accounts which will show them exactly how much grain is wanted in each place, how many people there are to be fed, what prices are being paid and where grain is plentiful.

There are so many wealthy merchants in India, all trying to make a profit by buying and selling grain, and it is so easy to send grain everywhere by railways and good roads that there is now no need whatever for government to buy grain in order to give away large quantities of it. In fact, as we have seen, more harm than good would be done if government acted in this way. It has also been found that it is not necessary for even private merchants to import grain from other countries. India is such a large continent that more grain is always grown in it than the people eat. In ordinary years what is not wanted is exported. In famine years it is sold in the country, and there is enough to meet all demands.

134. **Work and charity**. But, in a year of famine, the people who cultivate the land have no crops and no money with which to buy food. 'What is the use,' it may be asked, 'of merchants bringing quantities of grain to people if they have no money, after they have spent their little savings from former years or sold their jewels and there is nothing left?' This is where government comes in to help them. It does not give the people food. But it gives them money with which to buy food, or if they can work it gives them work, such as they are able to do, and pays them for it. In the famine year, 1897, there were in the month of June about 4,200,000 persons in India 'on relief.' Some of them were too old or too weak to do work of any kind. To them money was given without work. But a great many more could work. They were not able to do much, perhaps, but they could at any rate handle a spade or a pickaxe, or carry a basket full of earth. Some people may think that it would have been better to give them money without work. But work is just as good for the bodies and minds of those who need relief, as for those who are well and strong. It is also for the good of

government and for that of the rest of the people of India to get work done. The body, though weak, is kept in health by moderate exercise, and it is well even for famine-stricken people to feel that they are not beggars but that they are earning money to live on. There is also another reason for dividing these people into gangs of labourers. They fall into the ranks of a well-drilled army of workmen, and their health and the payment of their wages can be properly looked after. This is no small matter when many thousands of people are collected together in one place.

But the arrangement is also good for the people of India. The cost of famine relief is an enormous charge upon the taxpayers of India. When there is famine in a district, the usual revenue is not collected in that district at all, or is only paid in part a long time afterwards. Money, therefore, must not be wasted. Accordingly, when famine begins, there are, first of all, 'test works,' at which wages or relief are offered only to men willing to work. These show how far there is need for relief. So long as the wages paid are just sufficient to keep the workmen in health, it will not be necessary to give work to those who can support themselves by their savings or in any other way. Those only who are in actual need and can do nothing else to keep themselves alive will go to the government works. Thus money is saved not only by giving very low wages, only just as much as will buy food to support life, and by making men work to earn these wages, but money is also saved in the shape of the work done. When the 'test works' prove that relief on a large scale is really needed, then the workmen are sent to 'relief works.' Perhaps a railway embankment is built, a canal dug, or a reservoir made. The labourers are, it is true, weak, and their work is not worth the full amount of the wages which must be paid to them, but it is worth something, and this work is done for the good of the public. Relief in the shape of charity is always given to those who from age or weakness cannot work; but the rule that a few days' labour should be given by those who need relief and can work is just to the rest of the people of India, for it is from the taxes paid by them that the cost of relief is met, and it is of benefit as well to those who are relieved.

135. **Plague.** A sudden and terrible illness may now and then break out, which, like the 'black death' or the 'plague,' may, if it be not checked, destroy whole cities and bring ruin upon the survivors. At times like these it is the duty of government to help the people, to tell them what to do, and to place medical advice within their reach. In 1896 a few cases of plague appeared in the city of Bombay, and before many months had passed half the population had fled in terror, carrying with them to other parts of India the terrible disease which had attacked them. The plague, which by measures used in Europe might have been confined to a single city, was in this way taken to a great many places, where it spread among the people.

The effects of leaving a disease like the plague alone, to go its own way, ought to be carefully noted and remembered by everybody. In the first place, infection spreads and destroys human life, as a jungle fire burns down all that is before it, unless it be stopped. In the next place, the most distant nations, separated from India by continents or seas, take alarm, and refuse to admit either persons or goods coming from the infected districts until they have undergone special treatment. It sometimes happens that trade once interfered with loses its position, and the industries of many people in the infected country may be destroyed. As such mischief can be done by plague, it is the duty of government to do everything to stop it that can be done by man. It can open hospitals where those who are attacked may be taken in and nursed and treated by skilled doctors so as to give them the best chance possible of recovery. It can collect and publish information as to the spread of the disease and the best remedies against it. It can carefully examine people going by railway into a healthy city from places where plague is raging so as to prevent any of them who may be ill from carrying the disease into it. But the task of saving a whole population from death is too heavy for government unless the people themselves will help. This is fully understood in all civilised countries. Good citizens in India will in every possible way aid government officers, for by doing this they will save the lives of many fellow-citizens.

136. **Public markets.** Public bodies, such as municipal and local boards, can do a good deal to prevent or check disease. This is one of the chief reasons why self-government is given to a town or large village. Pure food is as necessary as pure water. But food is

sometimes sold in small, dark, dirty shops and in markets which are never washed. And milk is often made impure by milk-sellers who mix dirty water with it. Cholera and other diseases are spread in this way. In order that food which is sold to people may be kept clean, most municipal towns build public market-places, where traders can sell their goods in shops which are kept clean and have plenty of fresh air. These markets are regularly swept out, washed, and cleaned by servants paid by the municipal board, and it is the special duty of one of these officers to visit the market and see that this has been done. The local government of the town does not interfere with the traders in any way. They may sell what they please and charge whatever prices they choose.

In all these ways government tries to preserve the lives and health of the people, but government can never do as much for the people as they can for themselves. It is, therefore, the duty of every citizen to learn the value of cleanliness, and to be cleanly not only for his own sake but for the sake of his fellow-citizens.

CHAPTER XIII.

PUBLIC INCOME AND EXPENDITURE.

137. **Taxes, and why we pay them.** All of us, who live in India, pay taxes to government. Why do we pay taxes and what becomes of all the money that is

paid in the shape of taxes? How many different kinds of taxes are there, how are they collected, who collects them, how much money is paid to government in this way, and how does government let us know what it does with the money it takes from us?

We saw that in the oldest times in India each village governed itself. Every farmer or raiyat, at the time of harvest, set aside so many shares of his grain, so much for the headman, so much for the village watchman, so much for the priest, so much for the village servants, the barber, the weaver, the blacksmith, and so on. In later times, when there were chiefs and kings, a share was set aside for the chief or king of the country. Each of these shares was a tax, paid by each raiyat for some service done for him. The headman, in return for the grain given to him, was expected to see that all the old customs of the country which had come down from the forefathers of the village —the laws—were observed, and he settled all disputes. He did to some extent the work which is now done by courts of law and judges. The village watchman, in return for his share, took messages to other villages, watched the crops, kept off robbers, caught thieves and did what is now done by the police and the post-office. The chief or king in later times, in return for his share, kept up an army to protect the country from invasion.

The raiyat now pays taxes in money instead of in grain, the only difference being that a great deal more is done for him, and it is done much better than it could possibly have been done in former times, while the tax he pays is less than he ever had to pay before.

Every citizen of India pays taxes in return for services done for him. When you pay a tax, you are really paying certain men wages for serving you in some way. Out of every rupee which you pay, at the present day, you are paying the soldiers, sailors, and the police who protect the lives of yourself and your family from enemies, and enable you to do your work in peace by day and sleep in safety at night. You are paying for the roads and railways which make it so easy for you to travel about to any part of India and for goods from every part of the world to be brought up to your door; for the post and telegraph office, which take your letters everywhere; for the courts of law, the hospitals and the schools, all open to you, and for almost every comfort and convenience of life. For every pie you pay you get something in exchange. Some of the benefits or services rendered to us by Government are for our own special advantage, and others we share with other people. The water which a cultivator draws on payment from a canal, and the ticket which a traveller buys to carry him on a state railway benefit the payer of the charge imposed, while the public road is constructed and kept in order for the benefit of all of us. But one way or another it is true that without taxes we could not live, or at any rate our lives would not be worth living.

You and I and all the people of India are the public. The soldiers and sailors, the police, the postmen, the doctors, the engineers, the school-masters, and all the other men in government employ are public servants, that is, they are our servants whom we pay to do work for us—the pay we give them in the shape of taxes. It would be quite impossible for us to do for ourselves all the work they do for us. We should not know how to do it. And if we did, we should not have the time, for each one of us has to earn his own living, in the field, or in the shop, or at the office, or in some other way. Therefore all this work is done for

TAJ MAHAL.

us by others whom we call the government, or the servants of the public. Without the people there could be no government. Government exists for the good of the people. In helping government, therefore, we really help ourselves. Bad citizens who break the laws and the rules, which government has made for the good of all, injure not only themselves, but the whole body of good citizens.

As we saw before, it was not the custom in former times for the rulers of the country to give accounts to the people of what they did with the money they paid them in the shape of taxes. And no subject of a king would ever dare to ask him why he spent his money on this or that object. A great deal of the money was not spent for the good of the people at all, but kept hoarded up in the treasury. Some of it was laid out in buying jewels for the ruler and his family, or in building great palaces or tombs in large towns, usually the capital cities. No building was erected in small towns or villages far from the capital. A part, often a very small part only, was spent on the protection of the people and on public works such as roads and canals.

Our present rulers, however, give us full accounts of the different ways in which our taxes are spent. The money we give, we may call the public money, as we are the public. Those who represent the public on the legislative councils of the different provinces, or the local boards, or the Viceroy's council, and even the public newspapers, may freely give their opinions on the way in which government servants do their work and the ways in which the taxes are spent.

138. **Public Income**. The money which we, the people, pay—that is to say the taxes paid by the public —are the income or what 'comes in' to the government treasuries. On the other hand, the same money, which is spent for the public good by government, is called the public expenditure. Let us now see in what different ways government gets money to spend upon us and to supply our numerous wants.

In the first place government, acting for the people

of India, is the great landlord of the country. It owns the land except where it has given it to Zamindars, and those who cultivate it pay rent for it to government, as they formerly gave a share of their grain to the king. This rent is called the land revenue, and as by far the greater number of the people of India are cultivators of the soil, the largest part of the public income is land revenue. It is clear that those who pay this tax receive much in return for it, since they not only get the benefit of the services done for them by government, but also the use of the fields which give them work and a living. Government also makes and sells salt and opium, it carries letters by post, it makes and works railways and canals, and the profits that are made out of all these things are a part of the public income. Those who do not cultivate the soil, but buy and sell goods or make a living in other ways, also contribute a share of their profits to the public income in the shape of a tax. If money be wanted any year for public works, or to meet the cost of a famine, or for any public purpose for which there is not enough in the treasury, government borrows money from rich men who are willing to lend it, and pays them interest on it. Even if money be not wanted for any special purpose, government is always ready to take charge of the savings of poor men and pay them interest on them. In this way government does the work of a great bank for the whole country.

139. **Budget Estimates and Accounts**. The government of India begins its year on the 1st of April and ends it on the 31st of March following. This is known as the government or official year, to distinguish it from

the calendar year, which begins on the 1st of January. Thus the government year, 1903-1904, means the year from the 1st of April, 1903, to the 31st of March, 1904. It is sometimes written 1903-4. Before the year begins, government calculates what it expects it will get as income and what it expects to spend, during the year. This calculation is shown in a paper of accounts called the *Budget estimate.* After the year has begun, and as the months roll by, it is found that the receipts will be more than the estimate or that they will be less. Perhaps a famine occurs and the raiyats cannot pay their rents, or the profits from railways are less than it was thought they would be. Or if the receipts are more than the estimate, or even if they come up to it, it may happen that the expenditure is larger. A war may break out, or money must be spent on famine-relief. Government has in this case to decide that it will spend less on some object than it at first intended to do, or to borrow money to make up the loss.

If the receipts are more than were expected, government is able to spend more on something than it at first thought that it could, or it is able to pay off some of the money that it borrowed in former years. Those officers of the government who have charge of the public accounts and receive reports from all the treasuries in the empire, make fresh budget estimates accordingly, and before the year is closed, *Revised estimates,* in which all necessary changes are entered, are published. Finally, after the close of the year, and after complete accounts from the various provinces and districts have been received, and the accounts of the year have been made up, government publishes a third set of papers called the *Accounts*, which show how much money has actually been received during the year, and how much has actually been spent. In this way the public are informed what has been done with their money. For instance, a certain raiyat has to pay five rupees rent for the land he holds. This he has to pay not all at once, but in 3 or 4 parts or instalments, at different times in the year, as he gets money by selling his crops. This estimate is sent from the village to the taluk, from the taluk to the district, thence to the government of the province, and lastly to the Supreme government. Five rupees is accordingly entered under the head of 'land revenue' in the *budget*. But the early monsoon fails, and the raiyat, having no crop, cannot pay his first instalment of, say, 2 rupees. Accordingly, in the *revised estimate*, only 3 rupees are entered. But perhaps the later harvest is very good, and the raiyat gets a very large crop and is able to pay his full rent for the year, and so, in the *accounts* made up after the year has closed, 5 rupees are entered as actually paid. The accounts of India were formerly stated in rupees. Then they were shown in tens of rupees. But since 1900 they have been stated in pounds (£) at the rate of Rs. 15 to £1. A million pounds = one and a half crores of rupees.

140. **Taxes and rates.**—Taxes are direct and indirect. *Direct taxes* are taken directly from the persons intended to pay them. The man who, by paying Income tax, gives a share of his private income or of

the profits he earns by his work to government. pays a direct tax. So does he who pays a fee for registering a deed. *Indirect taxes* are paid to government by persons who after a time get back what they have paid from other persons. Persons often pay indirect taxes without seeing that they do so. Instances of indirect taxes are excise, customs, and tolls. The *Excise* is an indirect tax paid on articles which are made or produced in India, *Customs* are a tax levied on goods which are imported into India or exported, and *Tolls* are a tax for the use of a road, and are levied on articles carried along the road. If a petty shopkeeper sells European cloth in a village in the interior of the country, he must charge the buyer a price which will include the price of the cloth at the factory in Europe, and the charges for its conveyance from Europe to his shop, together with the customs duty paid in Bombay, and any tolls which have been paid on the road. To all this he must add his own profit, and the buyer pays the total, as the price. If it had not been for the customs and the tolls, the article would have been cheaper. Thus the tolls and customs make up the indirect tax, first of all paid to government by the merchant and then repaid to him by the buyer. The tax thus falls on the buyer, but because he does not pay it himself directly to government, it is called an indirect tax. *Rates* are taxes which local bodies such as municipal councils are allowed by government to levy for local purposes. Sometimes to save a local board trouble and expense, government collects for it a *local cess* or tax, for local purposes, which is a certain part, say, a sixteenth part, of the land-rent, but paid in addition to it. It is paid over to the local board, which spends it on its own district or taluk.

141. **Rules by which taxes are fixed.** In fixing the taxes which people have to pay, our government follows certain rules. In the first place these taxes are fixed by law. They do not keep changing from year to year. They are published, so that everyone knows exactly what they are. Every raiyat knows just what he has to pay to the tax-collector, and no more than this can be taken from him. A second rule is that the taxes shall be as few as possible, and that the money directly paid by the people shall, as a general practice, go into the public treasury and none of it be taken by those whose duty it is to collect it. In former days the collectors of rents were allowed to pay themselves out of the land-revenue, a part of which, sometimes a large part, they kept back for themselves. A ruler would often 'farm out' a number of villages to an officer, that is to say the officer had to pay a certain sum, say a thousand rupees, to the ruler, and might take as much more from the people as he could force them to pay. He might take one thousand, two thousand, or three thousand rupees as his share, if he could make the people pay. Sometimes the right to collect all taxes in a district, or part of a district was sold by auction to the highest bidder, and the more the successful bidder paid government, the more he compelled the people to pay. Nothing of this kind can be done now. The collectors of direct taxes are paid fixed salaries and must pay into the government-treasuries every rupee that they collect.

It is only in the case of a few indirect taxes that the system of contract is adopted, and then care is taken to fix by law the toll or the tax which the contractor may charge. Formerly, too, there used to be a great many trifling taxes or cesses in addition to the land-rent, which gave people a great deal of annoyance and often did not reach the government treasury at all. There were taxes on feasts, on marriages, on different kinds of food, on journeys and changes of residence, and many other things which have all been swept away. When the British government took the district of Coimbatore in South India, in 1799, after the fall of Tippu Sultan, they found that, in addition to the land-revenue and transit duties, there were no fewer than 61 different taxes. A third rule is that all classes, rich and poor, shall be taxed in the same way and by the same rules. There is not one law for the noble or great man and another for the poor raiyat. Each pays in proportion to the work that is done for him by government. A fourth rule is that as much as possible of the money taken from the people should be given back to them, that is to say, spent for their benefit on public works, such as railways and canals and roads, and schools and hospitals.

142. **Total Public Income**. Taking the year 1903-1904, of which *the accounts* have been published, the total public income was about 125·6 crores of rupees. But of this 1·2 crore was received in England partly for the services of troops lent by the government of India, partly from contributions paid towards pension by officers on leave, and from other sources. It is unnecessary to deal here with the sums received at

home, and we may proceed to examine the income of 124·4 crores which was collected in India as follows :

32·3 crores	from railway receipts.
28·8	from land-rent.
8·6	opium sales.
7·9	from salt-tax.
7·8	post, telegraph, and mint.
7·5	excise.
5·9	customs.
5·4	stamps.
4·3	irrigation under canals, wells, and tanks.
4·2	provincial rates.
2·4	receipts from civil departments.
2·2	forest produce.
1·8	assessed taxes.
1·1	interest on loans.
1·0	certain army receipts.
·9	contributions from native states.
·9	miscellaneous on account of pensions, etc.
·9	sale of stores for roads.
·5	registration.
Total 124·4	

Railway receipts. The Government has built many railways which are called state-railways, and the income from selling tickets to passengers or charges for carrying goods brought in nearly 31 crores of gross receipts. In addition to this the Government has guaranteed to certain lines built by companies a rate of interest even if their lines do not earn it, and in return it receives part of the profits if the lines earn more than the guaranteed rate. Besides this it makes advances to help other companies which are constructing lines, and it receives from time to time repayment of these advances. From these various sources it received more than 32 crores, of which, however, much was spent in the cost of working the lines.

The Land Rent. This is the rent which is paid, by those who cultivate land, to government which is the public landlord. In many countries, *e.g.* England, the land does not belong to government but to landlords who charge their tenants such rent as they are willing to pay. In India the government has always been looked upon as the owner of the land. The present rent is far less than would be charged by a private owner. This is clear from what we see for ourselves in India, for in some parts, *e.g.* Bengal, there are vast estates owned by zamindars. They have to pay a rent to government, but the rent they make their own raiyats pay, to whom they sublet the land, is much higher than what government would charge. The raiyats in South India and elsewhere who are the direct tenants of government pay much less rent for their fields than the raiyats under zamindars do, or the raiyats in native states. So long as a government raiyat pays his rent, he keeps his land. When he dies his sons keep it, and so do their sons if they continue to pay government the rent fixed on the land. Other people may be willing to pay a higher rent than the raiyat does for his land, but they are not allowed to disturb the raiyat so long as the latter regularly pays the rent at which Government gave him the land or agreed that he should continue to hold it.

It is impossible for a rich man to take away from a poor man his land, by offering to pay to government a higher rent. So long as a raiyat pays the fair and moderate rent fixed by government, the land is his, to cultivate. In some cases, indeed, the raiyat himself sublets his land at a profit. He pays to government the rent fixed and lets out the land to other tenants from whom he takes a higher rent. It is a good thing for the people of India that government owns the greater part of the land. The rent which government receives is a part of the public revenue and this enables Government to provide what the people require without raising taxes to meet the whole cost of it. All of us, who live in India, get some benefit from the land in this way, even though we may not cultivate it, for if it were not for the land-rent, we should all have to pay much higher taxes.

Opium, which grows well in India, is bought chiefly by the Chinese, and the large profits which are made out of this trade by government save us from the taxes which we should have to pay if government did not get this money from the Chinese. It must be remembered that we are dealing now with total, or gross, income, and from these receipts must be deducted the advances and other payments made to the grower of opium, chiefly in Bengal.

The salt tax. The salt used in India is either manufactured in the country or imported from other countries. The charge made by Government for every maund, 82$\frac{2}{7}$ lbs., was reduced in 1905 to Rs.1·8 throughout India except in Burma, where it is R.1. This rate is 25 per cent. lower than the rate charged at any date since the salt duties were made uniform throughout India in 1878. In addition to this reduction the salt manufactured by Government is made at so cheap a rate and so easily transported by railways that the cost of the article with the tax is far less than it ever was in old times without taking into account the duty at all.

Customs are the taxes paid on certain goods imported into the country or exported from it by traders. They are really paid, though indirectly, by those who buy these goods afterwards. Import duties were abolished in 1882, but reimposed in 1894 on the value of most articles imported into India except railway material, food grains, coal and some other raw materials. They are fixed at 5 per cent. on the value of the goods imported, except iron and steel, on which the duty is 1 per cent., and woven cotton goods, on which it is 3½ per cent. The chief export duty is on rice, and rice-flour, most of which comes from Burma, and is levied at the rate of 3 as. per maund of unhusked rice.

Excise is the tax put by government upon certain articles made in the country, *e.g.* liquor, toddy, opium consumed in India, and drugs. This, like the customs, is an indirect tax on those who use these goods.

Provincial rates or cesses. These are taxes raised by government for the most part on the land (in addition to the ordinary taxes) in some parts of the country for the benefit only of the people who live there. They are paid over to some board or council to be spent in the tract which they govern. They are also called local rates or cesses. They are entered in the accounts as provincial rates, because they are levied in some one province alone, and not over the whole empire.

Commercial services. The receipts from *railways, forests, post-offices, telegraphs*, and *irrigation*, which are given above, are not all profit, for from them must be deducted the cost of working these departments, which will be shown below. They are payments by those persons who use the railways and canals, or send letters by the post or messages by the telegraph, or buy timber from the forests. If government did not do all this work private companies would, and the people would still have to pay for the services rendered to them, but the profits would enrich the commercial companies, and not be spent as they now are for the public benefit. In all these ways the people of India benefit by the profits which government makes, because all these profits are spent for the good of the country, and the taxes are kept lower than they otherwise would be. How great is the advantage which the people of India derive from the railways and other public property which they possess may be seen from the fact that, although the gross revenue of 1903-04 was 124 crores, not one-half of this was raised by taxation.

Assessed taxes. These are the taxes levied on the income of the richer classes, there being no tax of this sort to be paid by those whose income is Rs.1000 a year or less. They are so called because the incomes liable to the tax are 'assessed' or valued in order that the amount of the tax may be fixed. The income tax is not levied on profits derived from agriculture.

The *civil departments* collect fines, receive fees paid by parents whose children attend state schools, and by the richer classes who attend hospitals or buy medicines; and sell stores of which too large a supply may have been received.

Stamps. Stamps on receipts, as well as stamped paper used for deeds and in courts and offices, give a large profit to government. These stamps are really a tax paid by the people who use the courts of law.

Registration. The fee which anyone pays for having a paper of any kind registered is really a tax paid to government. All the fees paid in this way are called 'receipts from registration.'

Interest on loans. This is the interest received by the government of India for loans made to certain native states, to municipalities and to landholders and cultivators.

If the total amount paid in the shape of taxes be divided by the total population of British India, it will be found that on the average each person pays a tax of 1s. 10¼d., or Rs.1 as. 6 p. 3 per annum, without including land revenue. If this be included the average taxation per head will be 3s. 5¼d., or Rs.2 as. 9 p. 3. This is much less than is paid in European countries.

143. **Public expenditure.** So far we have seen how the government of India gets money to spend on the country. We may now see how this money is spent.

There are two ways of looking at both expenditure and income. We may either look at the whole amount that is spent, which is called the *gross* expenditure under any head, or we may consider only the *net* expenditure, that is to say the amount which is left after taking from the total expenditure the income which government may get under that head. For example, in one province the gross expenditure on education may be 20 lakhs, but perhaps government gets back 2 lakhs in the shape of fees. The net expenditure under this head would in this case be 18 lakhs. Let us take another example. The gross income of government under post-office and telegraphs may be two and three-fifths crores of rupees, but it spent two and two-fifths crores on these departments, so its net income was one-fifth of a crore. It is clear that net income is the same thing as profit. We may either say that the net income of government from the post and telegraphs was 20 lakhs, or that government made a profit of 20 lakhs in working the postal and telegraph departments. Again, take the land revenue. The total receipts under this head may be 25·4 crores; but to collect this amount government may have to spend 6·3 crores; the net income of government from the land revenue would therefore be 19·1 crores.

144. **Gross expenditure**. Taking the same year, 1903-1904, for which the gross income was given above, the gross expenditure amounted to about 121·1 crores, of which 27·1 crores were paid in England. But since the revenues of India paid all the charges, we must consider the details of the

whole expenditure, which were as follows in round numbers:

Railways	- -	cost crores	31·0
Army services	-	„	26·8
Civil departments	-	„	18·0
Demands on and collection of revenue		„	12·9
Public works -	-	„	8·5
Post, telegraph and mint		„	7·7
Miscellaneous	-	„	6·5
Irrigation	- -	„	4·1
Interest on debt	-	„	2·4
Net provincial adjustment		„	1·8
Famine relief	-	„	1·4
		Total	121·1 crores.

As the gross revenue received both in India and in England amounted to 125·6 crores, there was a surplus of about 4½ crores, or nearly three millions of English pounds sterling, in 1903-04.

Railways. It will be seen that more money was spent on railways than on anything else. But although the large sum of 31 crores was spent in working expenses, interest on capital, etc., more than 32 crores were earned by these railways, and there was actually a profit of 129 lakhs of rupees.

Army services. Under this head is included the cost of the British troops and the Indian army which defend India, of the military roads and works, and the upkeep of the forts. This amount is therefore spent on the protection or defence of the people. It is, of all the items of expenditure, by far the most necessary, and as the empire grows richer and more envied by other countries it is likely to increase.

Civil departments. The most expensive of these departments is the police, but it is, next to the army, the most important. It costs us about 3¾ crores at present, and very large additions are being made to it. The money, however, is well spent, for without a good police force there would be neither safety nor comfort for the citizens of India. The other departments under this head are law and justice (3¾ crores), the jails and the various civil services, Imperial and Provincial, also education, the medical department, the ecclesiastical, the political and the scientific and marine. More than 2 crores of rupees were received back from these departments in the shape of fees and other receipts.

Miscellaneous. These charges included the cost of stationery and printing and of leave and pension allowances to government officers and political pensions. About thirty-eight lakhs of this expenditure was received back by government from officers who contribute a part of their pay towards their pensions.

Net provincial adjustment.—This is a sum given by the Imperial government to Provincial governments out of its funds when the share of revenue given to them is altered by a change of law, as in the case of the income tax, or when owing to famine, plague or other causes their revenues fall short of that which it was intended that they should have to meet their expenditure.

Famine relief. Government cannot altogether prevent famine, and famine costs a great deal both in actual relief, and because no revenue or very little is paid in those districts where there is famine. Government, therefore, now makes arrangements beforehand to meet the cost of famines which may occur. So a prudent father puts aside a portion of his income every year to meet the cost of medicines and doctor's bills in case any of his family should be ill. In its budget estimates every year government provides or 'appropriates' a sum for this purpose. If famine does come, the whole sum and as much more as is wanted is spent on the actual relief of famine. If there be no famine, the sum provided is prudently used either to pay off some of the debts caused by former famines, or to make a railway or canal which will protect from famine the country through which it runs. When a famine actually occurs, government, instead of raising the taxes in other parts of the country, again borrows money and pays off the debt from the famine relief fund of future years, in which there is no famine. If the money were put on one side and not spent, the interest on it would be lost and government would have to go on paying interest on its general debt. By paying off a part of this debt every year, government has to pay less and less interest to those from whom it has borrowed money.

Home-charges. The gross income as given above includes certain receipts in England, and the expenditure includes certain sums paid in England. The latter are called home-charges in the accounts. In this expression the word Home means England, and the home-charges are the money that the government of India sends to England to pay for various things which it has bought in Europe, or else to discharge its debts to its own officers on leave or pension, and to those other persons who have lent it money in time past. Thus the largest payment made in England, more than a third of the whole, is on account of the railways which, as we have seen, give a profit to India. The next is a heavy charge for the army, and after that the interest due on loans, and the payment of officers for work which they have done in the past or are still doing for India account for almost the whole of these three charges.

The public or national debt. About one-sixth of the home-charges in 1903-1904 was interest on the public debt. It is easier for the government of India to borrow money in England than in India, and a lower rate of interest is paid. When government has to borrow money, advertisements are put in the public papers, and anyone may offer to lend the money either in India or England. The interest which government gives is too low to induce natives of India to lend even one-third of the amount required, for they can get higher interest for their money by lending to private persons.

The government is constantly raising money for productive works, such as canals and railways, but it also owes money both in England and in India for loans raised to meet the cost of wars or famines from which no future profit can be expected. Part of its debt is *temporary*, and is paid off as funds are available; but another part is called *permanent*, because it is not considered fair that the present generation should bear the burden of paying it off and leave its successors no share of it. Every year large debts are discharged in payment of money deposited in savings banks or in courts of law, but a loan which was borrowed to enable India to gain a new province, such as Burma, is a permanent national debt of which future generations will reap the advantage, and it is enough for us to pay the interest on it.

The productive debt, or money borrowed to be spent on railways and irrigation works, is so called because

RAILWAY BRIDGE ACROSS THE JUMNA.

government makes a large profit out of these works every year. They add a good deal to the comfort of the public, they help the raiyat to cultivate and sell his crops, and they keep off famine. If it were not for them, government would have to borrow largely every year, and thus add to the unproductive debt. The actual profits made by them not only pay all the cost of working, but leave a surplus, out of which government is able to make new productive works instead of borrowing more money for this purpose.

At the present time the total national debt of

India amounts to 214 millions of pounds; but government possesses a property worth 250 millions. It has spent 88 millions on railways and 26 on irrigation works, beside buying railways at a cost of 85 millions —on all this expenditure it makes a large profit. Besides this, it has 20 millions in its treasuries, and 8 millions as a gold reserve, and has lent native states and companies 23 millions.

145. **Net expenditure**. We have now seen the whole of the income and of the outgoings of the government of British India. But it sometimes happens that a department of the administration earns more than it spends. Thus railways brought in more than 32 crores of rupees and cost the state 31 crores in the year which we have examined. The public gained a profit of one and a quarter crores, or, as it is expressed, the net revenue was the amount just stated. When we deduct all that the government received in its spending departments, such as post-office and railways, from the expenditure of these departments, and also deduct from the revenue of the earning departments the charges incurred on them, the net income of 1903-04 was 70 crores, and the net expenditure was 65½, showing the same surplus of 4½ crores which was the result of our examination of the gross revenues and expenses of that year.

146. **Credit of India**. The low rate at which the government of India is able to borrow money is a sure and certain proof of the prosperity of the country. To a bankrupt, no one in his senses would lend money at any rate of interest, whether

he was an individual, or a company, or a government. To any one who was in difficulties, if it were at all doubtful whether he could repay the debt, no one would lend money except at a high rate of interest. But to the government of India the rich men of the world are ready to lend crores of rupees, whenever it needs money, at a rate of interest at which most of the nations of Europe would be unable to borrow. They know well what difficulties the government has in a country where famine often prevails, and where wars must often be fought with the savage tribes on the frontier. But they also know that the accounts of the country are kept very carefully and may be trusted. And they see that year after year more money is spent on productive public works, which cannot fail to make the country richer. They feel quite sure that the interest on their money will be paid regularly. Every rupee which is lent to India at 3½ or 3 per cent. is a proof that the country is considered, by those best able to judge—to be rich, well-governed and prosperous.

147. **Exchange**. Most of the expenditure of government is made in rupees, *e.g.* all the soldiers and civil servants are paid in rupees. But government has also to spend a good deal of money in England, for besides the interest on the public debt which has been mentioned, all the guns and other things wanted for the army are made in England and must be bought and paid for there. In the same way, all the engines and material used on state-railways is made in England. The money used in England is gold. The money which has to be

sent to England to pay the various home charges must be in gold money. But all the revenue or income of the Indian government is paid to it in silver rupees, so that the treasuries contain only rupees. Thus the government of India has silver money, and must pay in gold money. It has to buy golden sovereigns with its silver rupees. The value of gold and silver is not always the same. Many years ago an English sovereign might be bought for 10 rupees. Then the value kept changing; it was sometimes more and sometimes less. It cost government a good deal to buy sovereigns with its rupees. At last the value of an English sovereign was fixed at 15 rupees, so that the value of a rupee was one shilling and fourpence, and this is still about its value.

Perhaps you will like to know how this was done. There are a great many more silver mines in the world than gold mines, and it is much more easy to get silver than gold. Any one who had silver might in former days take it to the government mints and get it made into rupees at the mere cost of the work done in coining the silver. As plenty of silver could be had, rupees were plentiful. But when those who held rupees wanted to get their rupees changed into gold sovereigns they bid against each other, and whenever the amount of gold for sale in the market was small they had to pay more and more rupees for it. In this way government was year by year obliged to pay a great many more rupees than it formerly did, to buy sovereigns with which to pay for the goods it bought in England. At the same time its revenue from rupees remained the same, and it could not increase the revenue without raising fresh taxes. This loss of government was called the *loss from exchange*, and it kept getting larger and larger, as more and more silver mines were opened, and more and more silver was taken to the mints and rupees poured into the market. Government could not lessen the supply of silver. But as no one except government may coin rupees, it could lessen the number of rupees. So it closed the mints to the public, that is to say, it refused to make into rupees all the silver that was brought to the mints. Only so much silver was coined as was considered to be enough for the wants of the country. This was such as to make 15 rupees equal to one sovereign of gold, or one rupee equal to one shilling and fourpence. This value is known as the rate of exchange. The number of rupees in circulation is now limited, and government no longer suffers the loss it once did. At the same time the value of the Indian rupee in relation to gold may be affected by causes, such as the course of trade, which government cannot control, and therefore a gold reserve fund is maintained in case of necessity. This fund amounted, on the 31st of March, 1904, to more than six millions of pounds invested in gold securities, so that, if at any time 15 rupees could not buy one sovereign, debts due in England might, for a time, be paid by the sale of these investments for gold coins.

CHAPTER XIV.

EDUCATION, JUSTICE AND PUBLIC WORKS.

148. **A choice of benefits.** A few years ago three gentlemen were travelling with the writer of this book from Poona to Bombay at a time when a breach had been made in the Great Indian Peninsula Railway by floods near Thana. One of the travellers was a Brahman official, the second was a Parsi lawyer, and the third a well-known Muhammadan merchant of Bombay. As they went along they talked about the different departments of the British government in India, and then went on to discuss the question as to which of these departments was the best. The Brahman gentleman thought that the system of public instruction, and particularly higher education, had been of more benefit to India than anything else that government had done for the people. The lawyer said that British justice was a more valuable gift than the university, colleges and schools. The former pointed out that it was in 1857, the very year in which the British government was engaged in suppressing the Mutiny, that it found time and money to establish the first university in India. The latter drew attention to the respect shown by the highest British officials to the law of the land. "What," said he, "could prove this better than the fact that not even the governor of a province, nor the Viceroy himself, will disregard a decree of the High Court, although the Court itself has to rely upon him to carry out its orders, even

when those orders are against his own wishes and prevent him from carrying out his own plans. Anything like this was never heard of before, nor would it have been thought proper or possible under any former government in India." Just as the Parsi had said this the train was moved on to another line of rails, and an engine passed by drawing a number of trucks full of workmen, tools and railway material, in charge of a British engineer. The Muhammadan, who had been silent up to this time, jumped up and, pointing to the train, said, "There, look at that; the best lesson which the British teach to us natives of India is that they show us how to do everything according to a regular plan, and thus they are able to act at once when anything goes wrong. In times of difficulty or danger they never seem to be at a loss. They see at once what is to be done, and they do it quickly, carefully and skilfully. The break on the line occurred this morning, and now, within a few hours, an army of native workmen is on the way to mend it under an officer who knows what has to be done, and will teach the coolies how to do it. The public works of India are the best school in it."

149. **Educational agencies**. Many people think that education can only be given in schools, and that it ends when they leave school. This is not the case, for if government does its duty its citizens are always learning by experience. The total number of boys and girls at school in British India is about 4¾ millions, and out of every hundred children who ought to attend school 73 do not. In school children are taught not only to read and write, but something

about the history of their country and what they owe to their neighbours and to the Government. But we must not think that school is the only place where lessons like these may be learnt. There are many lessons which grown-up men may learn by looking at the different ways in which a good government does its work. When we grow up we find out by experience, and not merely by reading lessons in books, what the officers of government are really doing for us. We pay the taxes, and we see on all sides of us courts of justice, schools, police, hospitals, and public works. Then we can ask ourselves questions, and answer them by our own experience. For instance, as we learnt in the first chapter of this book, every man has his rights. He has a *right* to expect that government will protect his life and property, and enable him to live in freedom, comfort and safety. This is the *duty* of government. Does it do it?

Does the British government keep us safe from the attacks of foreign enemies by land and sea, and protect us from thieves and robbers in our native country?

We have seen what government spends upon armies of soldiers and the fleet and the police, which defend India from foes without and foes within the country. If it would not make this book too large, an account might be given of the different ways in which arrangements are made in large towns for putting out fires by machines which lift up water to a great height and dash it on the flames, and of the precautions against fires in crowded streets. It might be shown how, when a great river gets very full, and looks as if it would burst its banks, every care is taken to prevent mischief, and how messages are sent with lightning speed over the telegraph wires to summon engines and workmen to the spot, and to warn people who may be in danger to escape, if after all a flood should come. In all these ways government saves life and protects property.

Does the government try to keep the people in health; to prevent disease; and if it should break out, to stop it from spreading from one place to another; does it employ doctors to cure such as may be ill, and to provide medicines for the sick?

The hospitals and dispensaries all over the country, the 'sanitary' or health departments, the arrangements for vaccination, the money that is spent to prevent the spread of plague, and the Dufferin fund—are the best answer to these questions.

In times of famine, does government let the people starve, or does it give food to the poor cultivators whose crops have failed and who cannot get work to earn money to buy food? And in parts of the country which are overcrowded and where, even though there be no famine from want of rain, there are so many people that some cannot get work even in good seasons, does government find work for them?

Ask the millions who have found work and food on the famine relief works. Ask the men and women who work in tea and coffee gardens, for whose protection and comfort government has made special rules; and the emigrants to distant colonies who find the work there which they cannot get at home; ask them whether they do not owe their lives, the food they eat, and the clothes they wear, to the government of their country.

Does government help the poorer classes of people to save money, and lend them money to buy seed and cattle for their lands?

Yes, government does this. In post-office and other savings-banks about 925,000 depositors have put in about seventeen crores of rupees. In no other country in Asia does the government help the poor to save in this way, and nowhere else in this part of the world do the people trust their rulers to repay what is entrusted to their keeping, as they do in India. The people of India had no chance of doing it under former governments. It is only lately that they have taken to the custom of putting their money into banks and drawing interest on it. In the old days men used to hide their money in the ground to keep it safe, or buy jewels for their women. As time goes on there can be no doubt that a great deal more money will be put into banks and the people get richer by the interest they will draw on their savings. Government makes *takávi* or 'helping' advances of money to raiyats, to assist them in cultivation, and it lends them money to sink wells or in other ways improve their lands under a law called the Land Improvements Act. It has also given help to agricultural banks which lend money at a low rate of interest. After very bad seasons, when the poorer raiyats have had no crops at all or very small crops, government remits or wipes out altogether the rent which is due. In the budget for 1902-1903 no less than 200 lakhs of rupees were remitted in this way.

There are a good many rules in the code of laws known as the Procedure Code or in the Dekkhan raiyats relief act for the protection of debtors who owe more money than they can ever possibly pay, and who would, in former times, have become the slaves of their creditors.

In these and a great many other ways, which cannot for want of space be fully described in this book, the government of the country treats the people kindly and helps them as a father helps his children. By studying them, the citizens of India can learn by experience their rights and duties. But there are five very important subjects about which something may be said. They are public justice, public works, the post office and telegraph, the press and schools.

150. **Public justice.** Before India came under British rule there were no laws which applied to all races alike, whether Hindu, Muhammadan, Parsi, European, or others. The Indian penal code applies to all alike. It teaches us that government treats all its subjects in the same way. There is not one law for one race or class and another for other races or classes. Whoever breaks the law is tried and punished under this code whether he be Hindu, Muhammadan or Christian. Every one who lives in the country knows that there is a court to which it is easy to go, where he will get justice if anyone should injure him in any way. And if he thinks that he has not been tried fairly, or that the judge has made a mistake, he knows that there

are higher courts to which he may appeal, when his case will be tried over again. He need be in no fear that the judge will take the part of his opponent, if he should be rich or powerful, for the law is no respecter of persons. The people of India know this, and they trust the courts of law. This is shown to be true by the large number of persons who go to court. Over two million suits were before the courts of civil justice in 1902, of which more than one-third were in Bengal, and about 1⅓ millions of cases were before the criminal courts. The courts in which these suits were tried were open to any one who chose to go in. The plaintiffs were there, and the defendants and the witnesses and their friends and any visitors who wished to see and hear what was being done. All these persons were able to observe for themselves how carefully and with what fairness the judges and magistrates tried the cases before them.

151. **Public works.** These works, constructed for the good of *the public*, that is, the people of India, are a good example of the way in which India is governed. The money which government takes from the people is spent upon the people. Great sums of money were spent by former rulers upon magnificent buildings which are the wonders of the world. Visitors come from Europe and America to look at the Kutab Minar at Delhi and the Taj Mahal at Agra. But our government spends the revenues of India on far more useful structures than these. No one can have any doubt as to whether the railways, bridges, canals and dockyards on which millions of rupees have been spent by the present rulers of

the country, are not far more useful to the people of India than the palaces of Agra and Delhi or the tombs of the kings at Bijapur. They are what are termed reproductive works. They cheapen the cost of taking goods from one place to another and in this way enable people to buy their salt, cloth goods and other things at a lower rate than in

MADRAS LAW COURTS.

former times when all goods had to be conveyed over the country in carts over bad roads, or on the backs of bullocks or camels where there were no roads at all. It has been calculated that the saving to the people of India, in carriage of goods by railways alone, amounts to 75 crores of rupees every year, while an immense trade has been created which could not exist if there were no railways. They thus make the people richer.

Cultivators may now send their grain or cotton or sugar to markets where they can get the best prices for the produce of their fields. Travellers can go for much less money, in a much shorter time, and in far greater comfort and safety, a thousand miles than they formerly could go a hundred miles. And when, at the present day, money is spent on splendid buildings, these buildings are not for kings, or governors, or rulers, but for the use of the people themselves. Both in Bombay and in Madras the most beautiful and costly buildings, erected by government, are the High Courts; and in both places the most splendid halls are those of the Universities, which are temples of justice and knowledge not for the use of any one particular race, or sect, or religion, but for the use of the public. And there is another reason why the public works of India are valuable to the people. They are themselves vast workshops in which thousands of skilled artizans and engineers are trained and taught how to construct and adorn buildings. These same workmen apply the lessons they learn in them to the building and improvement of the private dwellings of the people of the country.

152. **Railways** are perhaps the most important of all public works. They do what the strongest kings cannot do. A king who rules over subjects of different races and religions and castes cannot alter their customs and ways of thinking, but this is done, very quietly and gradually but very thoroughly, by railways. The various classes and peoples of India now mix more together and see more of one another in railway carriages than

they ever did before. At the end of March, 1903, there were 27,138 miles of railway open, and 3140 more were being made. The total amount that has been spent on the lines that are open is about 350 crores, and as these lines earn a good deal of money that is paid into the public treasuries, our taxes are considerably lightened by them; that is to say, we pay lower taxes than we should have to pay if there were no railways. Some of the railways belong to the government of India or to native states; and others have been built by companies under agreement with government—called a 'guarantee'—that if they should not pay a certain rate of interest—formerly 5 per cent. but now mostly 3 per cent.—government will pay the difference to them; or else they are built with the help of an advance of capital, or subsidy, lent to them by government on the security of the line.

Any one who has travelled by these railways must have been struck with the skill of the engineers and artizans who made the lines and built the engines, and must have noticed what clever and careful arrangements are made to work the lines so that the trains may run exactly at the time fixed and so that there may be no accidents. The whole of the line, particularly the bridges, must be carefully watched and kept in good repair. One of the lessons taught by the railways is the use and necessity of punctuality. Unless you are at the station in time to take your ticket and take your seat, you will miss your train. The train waits for nobody.

153. **Irrigation works** deserve separate mention

whether they be canals or tanks. Long before the arrival of the British, the people of India had found out the value of tanks and wells, and one or two canals had been made by former rulers of the country. But it was not in their power to construct canals as large and as long as those that have been

AQUEDUCT, GANGES CANAL.

made within the last fifty years. In those days engineers were not so skilful as they are now. The great discoveries of modern times had not then been made. And the constant wars which raged all over India left neither time nor money for great public works like these. Some of the canals made by British engineers run like long rivers through wide countries. For instance, the Upper Ganges canal, which cost 3 crores of rupees, is like a main river 460 miles long, and with its branches or channels, 4480 miles in length, distributes the water over 900,000 acres. The Lower Ganges canal is 100 miles longer. It cost nearly 4 crores and consists of 560 miles of main canal and about 2500 miles of distributing channels. In Madras the irrigational systems of the three rivers—Godaveri, Kistna, and Cauvery—have main channels, which altogether extend for 1720 miles and irrigate 2½ million acres. Other provinces make similar use of their rivers, and a large income is derived from canals. Like the earnings of the railways, the money paid by these canals lessens the general taxation of the country. The value, however, of irrigation works does not lie so much in the money they earn for the public as it does in the benefits they confer upon the raiyats, especially in seasons when the monsoon fails.

154. **Post office and telegraph.** India is such a vast country that it will take many years before every improvement that is possible is made in the arrangements for sending letters all over the country. But enough has been accomplished to make aged men, who remember how things were done in former days, wonder at this one of the many benefits that have resulted from uniting all the countries of this vast continent under one government, and of the peace that now reigns everywhere. The rate of postage for Indian post-cards is one of the cheapest in the world and confers enormous benefits on the people. In one year alone, in 1902-3, as many as 254 millions of post-cards were sent.

The government of India now sends mail-bags

with letters over 140,000 miles and keeps up 45,000 post offices and letter boxes. It carries safely 23 crores of rupees a year for the public in the shape

POSTMAN, BOMBAY.

of inland money orders. By means of the value-payable parcel post, it carries about 3 millions of parcels and pays more than 3 crores of rupees to the senders of the parcels from those to whom they are sent. It remits money in a few hours to the extent of a crore and a half by Telephonic Money Orders. The Postal department performs other duties besides that of carrying letters, for it sells quinine to the poorer classes and pays pensions to the pensioners of the native army. Besides the post office there is the telegraph, by which messages may be sent from one part of India to another, however distant, in a few minutes. There are now about 57,000 miles of telegraph lines open, with about 2100 offices sending about 7 million messages a year.

Who can estimate too highly the value of the post office and telegraph to the people of India? Just think how we should miss them! How much information, on every kind of subject, is taken by the millions of letters and messages that are carried over the country! A great deal of this information is no doubt true, but some of it may be false. One lesson that everyone must learn for himself is, not to believe everything that is told him, nor all that he reads in a newspaper We must think, we must judge for ourselves, we must inquire into the truth of a story before we accept it as true. This thinking, this inquiry, this finding out of the truth is now easy because there are so many ways of asking others who know the facts of a case. In former days idle tales and false rumours spread over the country. People believed them and a great deal of mischief was done. But now, a careful man, when he hears a story of this kind can easily find out by a letter or telegram whether it is true or false.

155. **The Press and literature.** What effect books and newspapers will have on the people of India when they are able to read more widely than they now are, we can only guess. There are very few books and newspapers printed in India compared with England. In 1902 there were 710 vernacular newspapers—in 21 different languages—of which 208 were in the Bombay Presidency alone. The largest circulation of any daily newspaper was 4000 and of a weekly paper 17,000. There were 575 magazines or periodicals, and 8393 books published, of which 7081 were in Indian languages. Nearly all of them were read in the large towns only, and not in the villages scattered over the country in which nine-tenths of the population live. In England newspapers are read in every village, and books are to be found in the cottages of all but the very poorest classes. When the people of a country are able to read and to understand what they read, they will insist on having good newspapers. They soon find out when a newspaper gives false news or uses foolish arguments and will not buy it.

In England the editors of good newspapers are often paid very large salaries, such as few even of the high officials of government get. This is not yet the case in India: so few people read newspapers that those who own them cannot afford to pay liberally for news or for articles written for them. The consequence is that the most highly educated men of the country, the ablest scholars from the colleges do not, as in England, become editors or authors. One reason why books and newspapers are so little read in India is, no doubt, because so few people are able to read. As education advances, when every village in the country has its school, and if the country continues to prosper as it is now doing, we may hope that there will be an enormous increase in Indian literature, English and vernacular.

156. **Education**. We may be sure that the government of our country, which does its best with the money it receives to encourage trade and commerce and industry of every kind, sets a very high value upon schools and colleges. If possible it would gladly provide for the people twenty times as many village schools as it is now able to do, out of the funds in its hands. But as there is not enough money at present to give every village a school, government is obliged to attend to three objects. It maintains a few large colleges and good schools to educate men for the various public services and the leading professions, and to serve as models of what good schools and colleges should be. In the next place, it gives money in the shape of grants-in-aid to all persons or societies who are willing to help in the great work of education by opening and maintaining good schools and colleges managed by themselves. Thirdly, government directs local and municipal boards to keep up schools of their own, and to aid private persons who maintain schools, just as government itself does. The Imperial government and local boards employ a large number of inspecting officers, whose duty it is to visit the schools, examine the pupils, and see that the teachers are properly qualified to do their

work, and that the school-houses and the various articles and books used in the schools are suitable.

157. **Government colleges and schools.** In India there are, as everyone knows, three grades of educational institutions—the primary school, in which instruction is given in the vernacular; the secondary school, in which English is taught; and the college, in which the students read for some university degree, and where their education is completed. The education given in

SENATE HOUSE, MADRAS.

secondary schools and colleges is either 'general' or 'technical.' It is necessary to teach a great many subjects in them, for some men like one thing and some another. One man is by nature able to do what another can never do well, however hard he may try. The wants of society, too, differ. The classes of people who live in India are many and varied, and education ought to fit pupils to take part in all the services and employments which the country requires. For these reasons government provides what are called technical, science, and art schools, of which there are about

11 hundred. They maintain medical and engineering colleges and schools; veterinary schools, in which boys are taught all about horses and cattle; agricultural schools, in which they are taught the methods of farming; and schools of art and industry. Whenever a new experiment has to be made, government leads the way, and especially in female education and the teaching of science it is necessary for this to be done, because otherwise no attempt would be made.

158. **Private enterprise**. But the main object of government in education is the same as we have seen to be the case in trade and famine relief, namely, to get as many persons and bodies as possible to take part in it. Education is a work which concerns everybody. It is a task so vast and so important that it is impossible for government to do it alone. To educate the 232 millions of people in British India, government needs the help of a host of fellow-workers who will give themselves wholly to the noble undertaking and devote to it their time, their money and their energy. Upon local boards the duty is laid of providing for the primary instruction of the children of ratepayers, either by opening schools themselves, or by aiding private persons to do so. Societies which wish to do good to the people, and men who wish to earn a living by teaching are welcomed and helped by grants-in-aid. By such means many agents are induced to assist, and they are as a rule men who give to their work their whole heart and time. Many of them work not for pay, but for the good of their fellows, and thus a great work is done which government by itself could never do.

At first, when government began to attend to the education of the people, it was necessary for it to show the way to others by opening schools and colleges of its own; but as time goes on it has been found that the money which government can afford to spend produces larger and better results when carefully applied to the aid of private enterprise. It is a great benefit to the people to give them schools, but it is a still greater advantage to them if they can be led themselves to spread schools and colleges through the land.

159. **Primary education.** To those who wish to earn a living by teaching, there is not the same inducement to open primary schools as to take up work in secondary schools and colleges. Men will readily pay well for education in institutions which prepare them for a university degree, for a degree is a valuable certificate which enables the man who has it to earn a living easily. Now that this is well known, men are ready enough to open and maintain secondary schools and colleges, where high fees are paid. But the parents of children who attend village primary schools are poor, and as a rule do not value instruction. The fees they are willing and able to pay are very small, and not enough to support a man and the family that depends upon him. If the children of villagers are to learn to read and write, the State must make it easy for them. For many years to come, the public funds must pay largely for primary education. In the countries of Europe, it is felt that education is so important that the State must provide primary schools for the children of all citizens either free of all cost

or at as low a cost as possible. India is of such great extent that if this were to be done the taxes would have to be increased, and our government has not therefore attempted to do it. It is quite certain, however, that no citizen can fully and properly do his duty to his fellow-citizens and to the government unless he can read, write, and count properly.

160. **Numbers being educated.** About 26 per cent., or say, a quarter of those who are of an age to be at school, now attend school. There are a little over 4 million boys, and about half a million girls at school. Of the whole number about 3,300,000 are in public primary schools, and about 560,000 in public secondary schools, the remainder being in private institutions. This result is hardly satisfactory, and yet the gross expenditure on education, including taxes, rates, fees and other sources, is about 4 crores of rupees, and in the present year large additional funds have been provided for its extension.

CHAPTER XV.

THE TRADE OF INDIA.

161. **Trade a proof of prosperity.** As we are citizens of India we ought to know something of the trade which the merchants of our country carry on with other countries. One of the best tests of the government of any country is the state of its trade. In the first place no country which is at war can do a good trade. Merchants will not send goods

to a port if there be any danger that they will be seized by the ships of an enemy. Neither do they care to trade with an ill-governed country, where their goods may be seized by the government, or taxed so heavily that there is no chance of selling them at a profit. And unless goods are brought into a country very few can be taken out of it, for it does not pay ships to carry goods one way and return empty. Also, unless merchants can sell goods in a country they cannot get money to buy goods in it to take back to their own country. Trade with another country is called commerce, and it includes exports, or goods sent out to pay for imports or goods brought in. When the imports and exports of a country are very large that country is prosperous, and the merchants who buy and sell get their profit. Great numbers of workmen also obtain employment in making the goods or growing the grain or other vegetable productions which are exported, and in carrying exported and imported goods to and fro and in shipping them.

162. **Total trade of India**. The trade of India with other countries is very great, and it has increased enormously under the British government, so that it nearly exceeds that of Canada and Australia combined. A crore, as we all know, is 100 lakhs. In 1840 the total seaborne trade of India was worth 30 crores; in 1857 it was 82 crores; in 1877 it was 171 crores; in 1900-01 it was 207 crores; and in 1903-1904 it had reached the enormous sum of 278 crores, being an increase of 15 per cent. over the previous year. Its trade by land with other countries hardly amounts to

14 crores. India's trade by sea and land is now larger than the whole trade of Great Britain was 50 years ago, and that was then larger than the trade of any other country in the world. The figures given above for 1903-1904 represent the private trade of the country, and do not include the imports or exports of government for public purposes. This private seaborne trade consisted of merchandise, and gold and silver, as follows:

Imports—Merchandise, worth 84½ crores.
Gold and silver, „ 32 „
Exports—Merchandise, „ 153 „
Gold and silver, „ 8½ „

Merchandise. Taking the merchandise, it will be seen that the exports were in round numbers worth 153 crores and the imports 85 crores. The exports consisted of various things grown or made in India and sold to other countries, being valued at 153 crores of rupees. The imports were various articles produced or made in other countries and bought by India, being valued at 85 crores. In other words, India paid for foreign articles which were valued at 85 crores by the importers, and received 153 crores for her own goods exported, assuming that they were correctly valued. The difference of 68 crores was partly spent in paying debts owed by India in Europe, and partly received in imports of gold and silver.

Gold and silver. The treasure imported by private persons was worth 32 crores, and that exported was worth 8½ crores. The difference or net value was therefore an import of about 23½ crores. This means that India received in gold and silver part of the price of the goods which she exported, receiving most of the rest in goods imported by private traders or by government on the public account. For we must remember that the exports of any country, being what it sells, must pay for the imports, or the things which it buys, and for which it must make payment to the foreigner who produces them.

163. **Bills of exchange.** A part of the payment was made in treasure which foreign merchants sent to India, but the greater part is not sent over the sea in gold and silver. The Indian merchants have to be paid in coin in India. At the same time the Secretary of State for India has to pay, in Britain, large sums of money for the home-charges, which have already been described in chapter XIII. This money has to be paid out of Indian revenues, and one way of paying it would no doubt be to send the money from India to Britain. But there is a better way than this. As the Indian merchants have to be paid in India, those who have to pay them do so as far as possible through the Secretary of State. A British merchant has, say, to pay 1½ lakhs of rupees to an Indian merchant. The Secretary of State has to pay some capitalist in England £10,000. As we know, £1 = Rs.15, so the English merchant pays the Secretary of State £10,000, and he gives the merchant in exchange a bill or order on the Indian government to pay him Rs.150,000. This order he sends to the Indian merchant to whom he owes this money, and the Indian merchant cashes it at a government treasury in India. In this way

all parties are paid, and the cost and the risk of sending money all the way from India to Britain and from Britain to India are saved. In the year 1903-04 the Secretary of State in Council paid no less than 36 crores of silver rupees in India, and received in London nearly 24 million pounds of gold for his bills.

164. **Imports**. These included articles of food and drink, metals and metal goods, chemical drugs and medicines, mineral oils, raw materials and manufactured articles.

Articles of food and drink. These were sugar, provisions, liquors, spices, salt, tea and a little grain. Of these sugar (about 6 crores) was worth more than all the rest put together. It is the third in value of all the imports, being exceeded only by cotton goods and iron and steel. The fact that all this sugar was consumed in India besides the large quantities grown in the country itself, is a proof that the country is prosperous enough to satisfy its wants in this respect.

Metal and metal goods. These were chiefly copper, iron and steel, to the value of over 9 crores. Machinery to the value of 3⅓ crores was imported for use in Indian mills, of which there are now 203 cotton mills, containing 47,300 looms and 5,200,000 spindles, and giving work to 197,000 persons every day, seventy per cent. of them being in the Bombay Presidency.

Chemicals, drugs and medicines. Chemicals were worth 59 lakhs, and drugs 68 lakhs. Under this head comes tobacco, worth 50 lakhs. This was largely in cigarettes, the import of which has increased 90 per cent. in the last 4 years, although a great deal of tobacco is grown in India. Some proof of the prosperity of the country is afforded by this item of its expenditure.

Mineral oils. Kerosene oil worth 3¾ crores was imported. This is less than it used to be owing to the increasing production of oil in Assam and Burma. The finer kinds still come from America, but there can be little doubt that in time India will produce all the oil wanted in the country.

Raw materials. These were, besides the metals already mentioned, chiefly coal and cotton. The coal worth about 38 lakhs, was less than a fourth of what was imported nine years ago. This is because of the large quantity of coal obtained from the mines in India. The import of cotton was small, being worth about 5 lakhs, and consisted of the finer kinds grown only in America.

Manufactured articles. By far the most important of these were cotton goods, usually called piece goods. India produces 3½ million bales of cotton fibre, each bale weighing 400 lbs. It exports 40 per cent. of it, chiefly to Japan, and uses 48 per cent. in its own mills, while 12 per cent. is consumed locally. If the village hand-weavers would improve their hand looms, and if more enterprise were shown in the working of factories by steam power on the European system, the country might make up the whole of the cotton goods required by its own people. At present cotton goods are imported to the value of about 29 crores, being a little over one-third of the value of all imported merchandise. The same may be said of silk goods, worth 1 crore 80 lakhs, which came from Japan and China, and of woollen goods worth 2 crores and 10 lakhs. Other manufactured articles were wearing apparel (21 lakhs), boots and shoes (28 lakhs), glassware, matches, jewellery, watches, books, and many other things.

165. **Exports**. These consisted nearly entirely of raw produce grown in India and sent to other countries, some of it, such as rice, spices, tea and coffee, to be eaten and drunk, and some to be manufactured into various kinds of goods, such as cotton and wool. These things were exported to countries all over the world, 27 per cent. to Great Britain, about 12 per cent. to China, 10 per cent. to Germany, and the rest to France, America, Japan, and other countries.

The most important articles exported were raw cotton (24½ crores), jute, raw and manufactured (20½ crores), rice (19 crores), seeds (14½ crores), wheat (11½ crores), cotton yarn and cloth (10½ crores), opium (10½ crores), hides and skins (9 crores), tea (8½ crores); and, of less value, lac, millets and grain, raw wool, coffee, timber, indigo, oils, spices, raw silk, and other things. Owing to the great increase of canals which have turned the deserts of Sindh and the Punjab into cornfields, India is able to supply Britain with nearly twice as much wheat as that received from Canada, and since the population of India is almost entirely rural and engaged in agriculture, the British market is of the utmost importance to the raiyats.

166. **Manufactures make a country rich**. A

great deal of the raw produce in the list of exports need never have left India if the people of the country could have made it up into articles for use. The country would have been much richer if this had been the case. As manufactures increase, employment is given to more and more people in towns where there are large factories and workshops, in which articles of merchandise are made up. At the present day the richest countries in the world are those in which there are the greatest trade and the largest manufactures. India grows all the food that is wanted for its inhabitants. The first necessaries of life—what every man wants and must have—are, food to eat, water to drink, clothes to wear, fire to cook food and to keep one warm, and a house to live in. There are, no doubt, other wants which arise in civilised countries. Without food, clothing, houses and fuel, however, men could not live at all. But men who live in cold countries want more clothes to keep them warm than those who live in hot countries; they also need better houses and more fuel. It costs very much more to live in comfort in a cold country than in a hot country. As the greater part of India is hot, men can live on much less than in the cold countries of Europe. In winter, in Britain, fires have to be kept up in every house, not only to cook food, but to keep men warm while they are at work. For the same reason, thick woollen clothes must be worn, and thick socks and good leather boots or shoes.

In most parts of India it is so hot that, except for cooking, fires are not wanted, and thin cotton clothes, which are very cheap, are worn by everybody, while the greater number of the inhabitants who live in the country wear scarcely any clothes at all, particularly when they are at work in the fields or elsewhere. They go bare-foot as a rule. For these and other reasons labour is very cheap in India. As it costs much less to live in India than in Britain, workmen are paid much less. As a consequence, if the Indian workman were as active and intelligent as the British factory hand, it ought to cost much less to manufacture goods in India than in any European country. At present cotton is taken all the way to Britain, manufactured at a much higher cost there than it might be in India, and then brought all the way back. If all the cotton grown in India could be made up in the country, all the cost of carriage both ways would be saved, cotton clothing would be made at a much lower rate, a great number of Indian workmen would earn their living by the manufacture, all the people of India, who wear cotton clothing, would be able to buy it cheaper, and would be so much the richer by the saving they would make. All the profits of the manufacture would also go into the pockets of the Indian capitalists, provided they had the courage to put their money into it, and the skill to manage and work the mills. At present most of the large industries of India are worked with capital supplied from Europe. Indian workmen no doubt get the wages wherever the capital comes from, and Indian purchasers get cheaper goods. And there is no reason why the profits of the manufactures should not be made by the wealthy merchants of India if they would take the risk.

The circumstances which have hitherto prevented the citizens of India from reaping the full benefits of their rich country, their large population, and the peace which they enjoy under the British rule have been the following. Only 10 per cent. of the population live in towns, requiring little and unwilling to combine for large industries. In the next place, the people cling to primitive methods and customs, having no desire to live better than or differently from their forefathers. And lastly, as H.H. the Maharaja Gaekwar of Baroda lately remarked, 'they do not trust each other.' Education will do much to improve the position, and although at present only one million out of nearly 300 million people are engaged in modern manufactures, and the higher classes lack the enterprise, scientific knowledge and taste needed for industrial pursuits, yet the citizens of India may look forward to the time when their noble country will take its proper position in the world, and turn its splendid resources to the fullest and best account. It has been the steady aim of the British Government to promote this result during the past fifty years.

CHAPTER XVI.

THE QUEEN'S PROCLAMATION.

PROCLAMATION, by the Queen in Council, to the Princes, Chiefs, and People of India (published by the Governor-General at Allahabad, November 1st, 1858).

Presented to both Houses of Parliament by Command of Her Majesty.

VICTORIA, by the Grace of God, of the United Kingdom of Great Britain and Ireland, and of the Colonies and Dependencies thereof in Europe, Asia, Africa, America, and Australasia, Queen, Defender of the Faith.

Whereas, for divers weighty reasons, We have resolved, by and with the advice and consent of the Lords Spiritual and Temporal, and Commons, in Parliament assembled, to take upon Ourselves the Government of the Territories in India, heretofore administered in trust for Us by the Honourable East India Company:

Now, therefore, We do by these Presents notify and declare that, by the advice and consent aforesaid, We have taken upon Ourselves the said Government; and We hereby call upon all Our Subjects within the said Territories to be faithful, and to bear true Allegiance to us, Our Heirs, and Successors, and to submit themselves to the authority of those whom We may hereafter, from time to time, see fit to appoint to administer the Government of Our said Territories, in Our name and on Our behalf:

And We, reposing especial trust and confidence in the loyalty, ability, and judgment of Our right trusty and well beloved Cousin and Councillor, Charles John Viscount Canning, do hereby constitute and appoint him, the said Viscount Canning, to be Our first Viceroy and Governor-General in and over Our said Territories, and to administer the Government thereof in Our name, and generally to act in Our name and on Our behalf, subject to such Orders and Regulations as he shall, from time to time, receive from Us through one of Our Principal Secretaries of State:

And We do hereby confirm in their several Offices, Civil and Military, all Persons now employed in the Service of the Honourable East India Company, subject to Our future pleasure, and to such Laws and Regulations as may hereafter be enacted.

We hereby announce to the Native Princes of India that all Treaties and Engagements made with them by or under the authority of the Honourable East India Company are by Us accepted, and will be scrupulously maintained; and We look for the like observance on their part.

We desire no extension of Our present territorial Possessions; and while We will permit no aggression upon Our Dominions or Our Rights, to be attempted with impunity, We shall sanction no encroachment on those of others. We shall respect the Rights, Dignity, and Honour of Native Princes as Our own; and We desire that they, as well as Our own subjects, should enjoy that Prosperity and that social Advancement which can only be secured by internal Peace and good Government.

We hold Ourselves bound to the Natives of our Indian Territories by the same obligations of Duty which bind Us to all Our other Subjects; and those Obligations, by the Blessing of Almighty God, We shall faithfully and conscientiously fulfil.

Firmly relying Ourselves on the truth of Christianity, and acknowledging with gratitude the solace of Religion, We disclaim alike the Right and the Desire to impose Our Convictions on any of Our Subjects. We declare it to be Our Royal Will and Pleasure that none be in any wise favoured, none molested or disquieted by reason of their Religious Faith or Observances; but that all shall alike enjoy the equal and impartial protection of the Law: and We do strictly charge and enjoin all those who may be in authority under Us, that they abstain from all interference with the Religious Belief or Worship of any of Our Subjects, on pain of Our highest Displeasure.

And it is Our further Will that, so far as may be, Our Subjects, of whatever Race or Creed, be freely and impartially admitted to Offices in our Service, the Duties of which they may be qualified, by their education, ability, and integrity, duly to discharge.

We know, and respect, the feelings of attachment with which the Natives of India regard the Lands inherited by them from their Ancestors; and We desire to protect them in all Rights connected therewith, subject to the equitable demands of the State; and We will that generally, in framing and administering the Law, due regard be paid to the ancient Rights, Usages, and Customs of India.

We deeply lament the evils and misery which have been brought upon India by the acts of ambitious Men, who have deceived their Countrymen, by false reports, and led them into open Rebellion. Our Power has been shewn by the Suppression of that Rebellion in the field; We desire to shew Our Mercy, by pardoning the Offences of those who have been thus misled, but who desire to return to the path of Duty.

Already in one Province, with a view to stop the further effusion of blood, and to hasten the Pacification of Our Indian Dominions, Our Viceroy and Governor-General has held out the expectation of Pardon, on certain terms, to the great majority of those who, in the late unhappy disturbances, have been guilty of Offences against our Government, and has declared the Punishment which will be inflicted on those whose Crimes place them beyond the reach of forgiveness. We approve and confirm the said Act of Our Viceroy and Governor-General, and do further announce and proclaim as follows:—

Our Clemency will be extended to all Offenders, save and except those who have been, or shall be, convicted of having directly taken part in the Murder of British Subjects. With regard to such, the Demands of Justice forbid the exercise of mercy.

To those who have willingly given asylum to Murderers, knowing them to be such, or who may have acted as leaders or instigators in Revolt, their lives alone can be guaranteed; but in apportioning the Penalty due to such Persons, full consideration will be given to the circumstances under which they have been induced to throw off their allegiance; and large indulgence will be shown to those whose Crimes may appear to have originated in too credulous acceptance of the false reports circulated by designing Men.

To all others in Arms against the Government, We hereby promise unconditional Pardon, Amnesty, and Oblivion of all Offence against Ourselves, Our Crown and Dignity, on their return to their homes and peaceful pursuits.

It is Our Royal Pleasure that these Terms of Grace and Amnesty should be extended to all those who comply with their Conditions before the First Day of January next.

When, by the Blessing of Providence, internal Tranquillity shall be restored, it is Our earnest Desire to stimulate the peaceful Industry of India, to promote Works of Public Utility and Improvement, and to administer its Government for the benefit of all Our Subjects resident therein. In their Prosperity will be Our Strength; in their Contentment Our Security; and in their Gratitude Our best reward. And may the God of all Power grant to Us, and to those in authority under us, Strength to carry out these Our Wishes for the good of Our people.